NO MEAN FEAT

Dream Big.

NO MEAN FEAT

MARK INGLIS

RANDOM HOUSE
NEW ZEALAND

National Library of New Zealand Cataloguing-in-Publication Data

Inglis, Mark, 1959-
No mean feat / Mark Inglis.
ISBN 1-86941-536-1
1. Inglis, Mark, 1959- 2. Mountaineers—New Zealand—Biography.
3. Amputees—New Zealand—Biography. 4. Athletes with disabilities—
New Zealand—Biography. I. Title.
796.522092—dc 21

A RANDOM HOUSE BOOK
published by
Random House New Zealand
18 Poland Road, Glenfield, Auckland, New Zealand
www.randomhouse.co.nz

First published 2002, reprinted 2002

ISBN 1 86941 536 1

Design and layout: Kate Greenaway
Cover design: Matthew Trbuhovic
Cover photographs: Front cover: Mark Inglis (top and bottom left); Gareth Eyres/*North & South* (bottom centre); Grant Stirling (bottom right). Back cover: Mark Inglis.
All photographs reproduced in this book are supplied by the author except those otherwise credited to Gareth Eyres/*North & South*, Mary Hobbs/*New Zealand Outside*, Grant Stirling, and *New Zealand Herald*.

Printed by Publishing Press Ltd, Auckland

CONTENTS

To Anne, Lucy, Jeremy and Amanda,
Mum and Dad,
thanks for all the years
that have been and those to come.

AUTHOR'S NOTES AND ACKNOWLEDGEMENTS

WRITING THIS HAS BEEN a very personal experience for me, delving into my memories of the past 30 or so years. I have written this account of aspects of my life and experiences from memory, not always the most reliable source I'm sure, so I apologise if some people remember events differently.

It is also not a comprehensive documentation of my life, there are many events and people I have left out, it is rather my interpretation of this life, this 'work in progress' that I am.

Thanks are due to innumerable people, only some of whom are listed here. Bob and Anne Munro for the use of his words and the friendship of the whole family. Montana for teaching me so much over the years. AMP for their faith in me, supplying some tools for success, especially for the advice and help from Martin and Joan. Mountain Designs and Suzuki for both stepping up when others shrunk away. Charlie and Mary, Whetu, Spoon, Woody and Narly for reminding me what real life is all about. Wayne for his really weird thoughts and fantastic legs.

Chas, Hamish and the doco crew for giving me the vehicle to show New Zealanders this country of ours. Gnome for all those years of phone calls on 29th November, lots more years to come, mate.

Special thanks are due to Christine Thomson and the Random House team, for their expertise and teaching me a new skill.

Lastly (for now), thanks to my family, to Mum and Dad — stay well — to Anne, Lucy, Jeremy and Amanda — we have lots to fill in the next few years, let's do it all together.

1 MIDDLE PEAK HOTEL: BOOKING IN

JUST IMAGINE A SMALL home freezer, one that you can't quite lie down in, can't quite sit up in, and with a bit of a bend in the middle. Now prop the lid partly open and have a fan blowing some ice crystals in continuously. Set the temperature to about -10 to -20°C. Put an empty climbing pack and your climbing rope on the bottom and hop in.

Welcome, you are now in 'Middle Peak Hotel', my home for 13 days in late November 1982.

So, how do you book in?

For that we need to go back quite a way, as far back as when I was at primary school (All Hallows in 'Sleepy Hollow', a.k.a. Geraldine, South Canterbury). I will always remember playing my first games of rugby and hockey, thinking there has to be safer sports than these, sports where you rely on yourself, not others. It's not that I was critical of others in the team, more of myself. Crawling out from under my first ruck just strengthened my resolve to find another sport. Hockey seemed the go, but those sticks sure gave the shins a hammering.

Yes I know, toughen up, but you have to realise I don't mind doing damage to myself, but hate others having a go as well.

It was at Geraldine High School that I first got the chance to escape the traditional New Zealand team sports thing and go tramping and climbing. The school and I were lucky to have two teachers passionate about the mountains — Bert McConnell and John Blundell. It was the enthusiasm of people like Bert and John, and others such as Peel Forest resident artist, Austin Deans, that helped nurture my growing passion for adventure, for the mountains. One of my traits that may become obvious as my story unfolds is that I tend to get a bit passionate, perhaps even obsessed, about my projects: always have, always will, I hope.

And as my passion for climbing developed, the school's Tramping and then Alpine Club became a focus of my youth. School-organised trips (I did geography right through school — better field trips that way, studying the mountains and glaciers) took me to mountain ranges such as Arthur's Pass, Mount Somers, Four Peaks, Two Thumb, Mount Arrowsmith and, of course, Mount Cook.

With 'partners in crime' Ross Stevens and Shane Edgar, long weekends and holidays were for the hills. The trips were real adventures for 16-year-olds, heading into ranges we had only read about, frequently in awe of the pioneers of the Southern Alps and the climbers of the 1970s.

I quickly came to realise that I wasn't a born tramper, the concept of walking for days on end wasn't too bad, but what I really craved was topping out on mountains and the intensity of technical climbing. Early tramping trips always got turned into a climb of some sort and frequently into a race as well. I was rarely the fastest and rarely the slowest, far from being a great athlete I was a scrawny kid, but one who knew what he wanted.

Mum and Dad (Mary and Jim) worked very hard to provide for their kids. I was the youngest, with Anne the oldest and John in between. Both Mum and Dad worked: Mum in clothing shops, and Dad, for most of my youth, as a driver of trucks and graders. He had spent many years shearing, so the concept of hard work was no stranger to him or the family. We were never affluent but we never missed out on any essentials either. Early on in my tramping career I can remember needing an oilskin jacket. I had tried using two light nylon jackets and various other schemes but there was no avoiding it, to carry on with tramping and climbing I really needed an oilskin, and so they bought it for me, even though at the time it was a significant expense for the family.

My passion for climbing was matched only by my passion for motorbikes. Within days of my 15th birthday and gaining my licence I had the first of many bikes, small road bikes first, then trail bikes that became progressively larger and faster. The money for them had to be earned though, just the same as for Anne and John and their interests. I was lucky enough to be able to pick 'spuds' in the holidays, big business in South Canterbury, and in the 1970s still reliant on hand-picking of the potatoes into wicker baskets and then into bags. Many cold frosty mornings were spent stooped over the damp sticky earth — every spud got me closer to another motorbike, another ice axe or another day skiing — such powerful motivation. I probably spent far too much money on magazines, especially motorcycling and climbing ones. I had hundreds of them. I could get lost for hours, absorbing all the technical information (I was a gear freak from very early on) and dreaming of faraway places and races. Visualisation is a critical part of modern sports psychology, and I was doing it from my earliest years — it was just called daydreaming in those days.

Farm work also played an important part both in earning the money necessary to take those daydreams and turn them into reality and also in making me appreciate what real work is. I was privileged to work for a fantastic family, the McDonalds, near Peel Forest. Bruce and Hilary provided the benchmark for hard work and integrity. You always knew Bruce would never make you do something he hadn't done himself, and often he would show you what to do — that was the minimum, you should do better if you could. Another attraction was that the farm was just below the peaks of Mount Peel, snow covered and glistening in winter, always tempting.

With Mum working to help support the family, her kids would end up doing some of the cooking for tea every night, the start of a lifelong love affair for me, and an independence many kids don't attain until much later in life. Typical of Mum, 'cooking tea' for us was more a matter of turning elements and ovens on, as she is so efficient that it would all be set out in the morning before she went to work.

Coming from a background of needing to be careful with money, but still lucky enough (through Mum and Dad's hard work) to get plenty of treats, such as occasional family holidays and some financial help with those earliest dreams, there was ingrained in me the value of earning, of earning the right to achieve. It's that earning that was the essence of climbing for me, of doing the hard work and reaping the benefits, of gaining respect from others you respect.

The first real summit climbed by our small team (Ross, Shane and myself) was Mount Arrowsmith, 2781 metres above the Canterbury Plains. The Arrowsmith Range has been the traditional training ground for Canterbury climbers before they head to the big peaks of the Mount

Shane and Ross on Mount Arrowsmith, 1976.

Cook region. To get there involves hours of load-carrying up the Cameron Valley to the small hut hidden at the base of a glacial terminal moraine. A spectacular place, but freezing more often than not and with limited daylight hours, as it is in a canyon with the peaks of Jagged and Arrowsmith towering above.

It was here we got our first real introduction to travelling on glaciers and moving roped on steep ice and rock, with abseils back down — the real McCoy. It was climbs like these, at the edge of our experience and skills, that first gave me the hint of what was to come, what was possible. The essence of climbing has always been overcoming the inner self as much as the mountain. Those climbs that you look back on and really admire are frequently those that scared you shitless while doing them. So often, from tramping to high alpine climbs, I've got to the crux or the top and thought, 'How the hell am I going to get out of this?'

Leaving the Cameron Hut in the icy pitch-black cold of 3 am, we wound our way up the lateral moraine of the glacier by torchlight, navigating in the dark by coming upon landmarks we had seen the day before or had just read about. Daylight found us in the glacial cirque below the East Face of Arrowsmith. Our route went up the ever-steepening head wall of the cirque, moving over sparsely crevassed slopes to the bergschrund. It involved the usual tentative acrobatics over delicate snow bridges and up steep, firm snow to the crux pitch of mixed rock and ice. The pitch was in a gully which opened out onto the slopes leading to the summit ridge. Climbing roped was slow, with three on the rope, one leading and two following. The techniques used had been learnt on New Zealand Alpine Club training days and from our mentors. They were techniques that probably seem overcautious to young climbers now, but we learnt through trial and error, more trial than error luckily. It did make for slow learning, but the lessons stuck; we were safe climbers, suitably respectful, or perhaps fearful, of the mountain environment.

Standing on top of Mount Arrowsmith your eye is drawn to one peak — Aoraki/Mount Cook. It stands proud and commanding, the bulk of its massif is the dominant feature of the Southern Alps. Talk about whetting your appetite!

Every month a group of us from Geraldine would travel to Timaru for the New Zealand Alpine Club meeting to hear talks and see slide shows from climbs around the world. We used to feel very much the new boys on the block and, along with other young climbers like Charlie Hobbs, we would soak up the information and experience.

Some sessions were out at Mount Horrible, south-west of Timaru, a rock escarpment that had the best rock-climbing routes in South Canterbury. It was from experienced climbers there that we learnt the safety rope skills that we took with us when we first ventured into the high alpine environment of Mount Cook National Park. It was 1977, and Ross, Shane and I were 17-year-olds heading for the top of Mount Cook. Based at Unwin Hut, the New Zealand Alpine Club base near Mount Cook Village, we waited for the weather, like everyone else. Our plan was essentially the same as the one climbers use today: utilise the Mount Cook Airlines ski-planes to land us on the Grand Plateau at 2210 metres, 1544 metres below the summit of Aoraki/Mount Cook; the usual midnight start from the Plateau Hut, weaving up the Linda Glacier, thankful that you can't see into the crevasses that would swallow a car, or even a whole house, into their blue-green depths.

As always on Mount Cook, the weather rules, and in 1977, the summiting by three 17-year-olds wasn't to be; the westerly winds had picked up and as we stood at the base of the summit ice cap we had to make that painful decision to turn back. Close, so close you can see the top only 100 metres or so above you. The temptation is great — but so is the power of the wind.

Abseiling back down, weaving through the steep soft snow and yawning crevasses of the Linda Glacier requires as much, in fact more care than going up.

That trip was my first walk out from Plateau, not something to be done too often, I can assure you. That trip finished in a nor-west storm, the three of us arriving back at Unwin like the proverbial wet rats after walking the whole way out, over 20 km of glaciers, steep broken rock, scree, seemingly endless moraine and the monotonous Ball Hut Road.

Missing the last bus on the road turned it into a real marathon effort.

From those beginnings in 1977 climbing became the focus of my life (along with motorbikes of course, but that's another story). University lasted all of two weeks for me, I think — it didn't give me enough time to train and climb, so I was out of there. I spent 1978 working on farms and climbing: rock, alpine, anything.

With a climbing career in mind, I enrolled for the Diploma in Parks and Recreation at Lincoln University — the park ranger option of course. My ambition was to get a placement at Mount Cook National Park; the concept of being a climbing ranger seemed too good to be true. After six months at Lincoln I got my wish, my first work experience as a trainee ranger was going to be at Mount Cook. The idea was that you did half the first year in a national park to gain a better understanding of your academic study. Unfortunately what I saw was that my dream job wasn't to be a ranger at all, but one of the park's mountaineers. So it was goodbye to study and the start of what I guess you could call a 'boy's own' job.

Life at Mount Cook in the late seventies and early eighties was dominated for me by climbing, skiing and Search and Rescue (SAR). The combination of your job, your culture and your sport all wrapped up in one, with the added excitement and job satisfaction of SAR, is one that few 20-year-olds ever get to experience.

The three years at the park seem a blur, summers of climbing and rescues, winters of ski patrol on the Tasman Glacier, snow clearing in the village, heli-skiing in the weekends.

Three climbs typify those years for me: a Grand Traverse of Mount Cook via Zubriggens Route and the West Ridge with Malcolm Wood in 1980 and two climbs with Richard Pears in 1981 on Nazomi and Mount Hicks.

Nazomi is the peak just south of the Low Peak of Aoraki/Mount Cook. At 2925 metres it has a number of relatively short routes on good rock out of the Noeline Glacier under the South Face of Cook. Getting there is sometimes harder than the climbing. Entrance to climbs in the upper Hooker Valley involve an arduous trip up the Hooker Valley,

Nazomi, 1981: bitterly cold, frozen rope and body in the early morning.

dropping down onto the glacier just past Hooker Hut, then moving up moraine and white ice to where the glacier curves around Pudding Rock. Gardiner Hut, effectively a grain silo lying on its side and fitted out with a plywood interior, is perched atop the rock like a sentinel guarding the entrance to some of New Zealand's premier climbs. In the summer months it is rarely possible to move up through the glacier's tortured icefall, so it's up the Pudding Rock itself. While the rock is straightforward, with handy permanent wire ropes in places, it's getting onto the rock that can frequently challenge even the best climbers.

On my climb with Richard Pears, it was the next stage, moving up the crevasses of Noeline Glacier in the breaking light the morning after reaching Gardiner Hut, that is a time I will always treasure — the light on Mount Sefton to the west looked as though it belonged in a movie. We intended to have a look and choose a route, preferably a new one, out of the upper canyon of the Noeline near the Gledhill Buttress.

The route we chose doesn't even rate in guide books — I think we called it the Glot Buttress — as basically it went up a delightful rock rib near the Du Faur Ridge. My enduring memory of the climb was the intense cold, which actually froze the rope, turning it from a supple 10.5-mm lifeline to something akin to a wire rope. Damn difficult to manage, hands freezing, body stiffening in the cold. It's amazing how the lack of sun can turn a relatively easy alpine rock route (3+ or so I guess) to a shivering chore. As soon as the sun hits, there is an almost magical transformation, the rope thaws and away you go. We topped out on the summit ridge of Nazomi then scuttled back down (abseiling, down-climbing and glissading to the glacier) before the afternoon sun could soften the ice cliffs on the South Face of Cook, causing chunks that can be as big as cars to rattle off — it's not good for your health to be in the way of those.

Mount Hicks with Richard in the summer of 1980 was one of the few first ascents I've done. Up past Gardiner again — I have always loved the upper Hooker, such a dramatic place, but you sure have to work hard to get there. A few hours above Gardiner, under the Sheila Face of Aoraki/Mount Cook, is Empress Hut. Not much bigger than a dog box back in 1980, this was the base for many of the real extreme alpine routes of the seventies and eighties. Our goal was to go over

On the summit of Nazomi looking out onto the Caroline Face and East Ridge (skyline right) of Cook.

Harper Saddle, then to do something interesting on or near the North Face of Hicks. Getting over Harper Saddle was pretty straightforward even in the obligatory darkness. Just the one big bergschrund to do some gymnastics over and you're on the West Coast. Red Wall, our grade 4 rock route between the standard Curtain Route and the North Rib was, I'm sure, as much being partly lost as the desire to forge a new route. Richard was always superb on the rock — tall and athletic, he always made me look like a bit of a klutz stumbling along behind. Eight pitches (the full length of a climbing rope, approximately 50 metres) of warm (once the sun was up) good rock, one of the most elegant climbs I've done, I think. Great exposure (climbers' term for nothing below your feet for a very long way) to the upper La Perouse Névé, bright blue-white below. We topped out on the last part of the North Rib, on up to the summit ridge. Hicks is fantastic, as it really is a classical knife-edged ridge, rising in steps to an indistinct summit. It's one of those mountains that when you get to the top, the first thing you think is that it was hard enough getting up, how do you find your way off!

Down, in this case, was a series of abseils (five of them I think), down the couloir next to the Curtain Route. As always we were looking at ways of leaving as little gear behind as possible, not necessarily for the aesthetics of our high alpine environment, but more because we were typical frugal Kiwi climbers.

The following summer saw my first Grand Traverse (GT) of Aoraki/Mount Cook. Up until the sixties a GT of Mount Cook was still recognised as one of the most impressive achievements in world mountaineering and New Zealand's highest and most exposed mile is still demanding and spectacular today. As usual for me, our GT was not the more standard Hooker to Plateau but the reverse. Zubriggens Ridge was our route to the High Peak, steep snow and ice slopes up the edge of the East Face, a technical ice pitch at the ice cliffs 400 metres up the route — almost vertical for five metres. The slopes above allowed us to relax back to just plain calf-searing front pointing, joining the Linda Shelf just below the summit rocks. Up the rocks on a perfect summit day, or at least as near as you'll ever get to it on Cook (10–30 kmh westerly blowing). You never get sick of standing on Aoraki, higher than anything in New Zealand, looking down the great sweep of the summit ridge, to Middle Peak (yet to be termed 'Hotel'), to Low Peak, then nothing until the Tasman Valley and Lake Pukaki over 3100 metres below. Climbing off the High Peak is exhilarating to say the least, the first three pitches steep with great exposure. Gradually the slope eases up, either that or you become used to it, then a careful traverse on the jagged hard ice sastrugi, over Middle Peak, down to Porter Col. Back to fixed pitches on the gnarly mixed rock, snow and ice to the Low Peak. Once there we knew it was in the bag, we'd been on the go for over 12 hours, fast, but still a long time. The descent of the West Ridge to Gardiner Hut in the Hooker Valley was one of great care, with the GT finishing in the dusk, 19 hours in all. No flying out of the Hooker, but the walk out worth every step, especially in the Tavern Bar hanging on to a cold beer.

Those were the real highlights of what were golden years for me, my life embedded in the whole matrix of life at Mount Cook, with its enduring friendships and relationships, parties, and both monotony and excitement.

It was from the Park Headquarters that I first spied Anne. I'm sure it was the cowboy-style boots that caught my eye and not the fact that she had a car and I only had my XR500 motorbike, with winter coming. We both used to get a lot of ribbing from our friends: Anne for going out with a 'Parkie' or a 'smellie'; and me because all the guys at the park would take one look at Anne's red hair, shake their heads and ask me if I knew what I had let myself in for. We became part of another institution, another Mount Cook marriage. Then Lucy came along in January of 1982. For Anne, living at Mount Cook meant always needing to be pretty independent, and living with me made it even more so at times. Always on the go in every direction, I wasn't (and still am not) the classic helpful hubby. Sure I spent my fair share of nights up with Lucy, before the time of all-night TV and Sky I might add, but if there was a great trip on, then it was hard to hold me back.

Winter 1982, Anne and I were house-sitting for Bert Youngman, the

Chief Ranger. A beautiful old stone and wooden house, one of the earlier National Park houses perched on a bank up near the Hermitage with a prized view of Aoraki/Mount Cook's South Face. Winter with a new baby meant the fires were always burning. I had just taken out an old chimney and installed a new wood-burner in the lounge for Bert and we also still had a coal range in the kitchen, essential for all those winter power cuts. As luck would have it I was rostered on Ski Patrol (on the Tasman Glacier) on a day with a fresh fall of new powder. I was up early and bursting out of my skin to put tracks down fresh powder at the head of the glacier, a perfect day, one you dream about. Driving down to the airport I looked behind, back up towards the village, to our house on the bank, only to see smoke and flames coming out of the coal-range chimney. Decision time, do I go back and deal with the chimney fire or leave Anne to it — just then the fire siren sounded and I knew she was in good hands. It was only a chimney fire after all, and it was great powder — easy decision really.

Summer 1982, I was given the chance to lead one of two Search and Rescue teams for the Mount Cook National Park Board as it was then (now DOC). Lindsay Bell, normally one of the two team leaders with Don Bogie, was heading for Antarctica for the summer season, so I was given this fantastic opportunity. The summers brought climbers and trekkers from around the world, to be advised, hosted and sometimes rescued. One summer alone I think we did 33 rescues, a mixture of the minor, the serious and the fatal.

Don Bogie was the senior mountaineer, a powerful climber and one of the most experienced Search and Rescue climbers in New Zealand. The teams were comprised of both permanent park staff and 'summer mountaineers' hired to help with every facet of park life, from track and hut maintenance, to talks and walks, to SAR.

That year I had Phil Doole as part of my team. Phil, a surveyor with the Lands and Survey Department, had been climbing in and around the Mount Cook region for many years. In fact several years earlier he had himself been involved in a rescue situation. While descending the Linda Glacier Phil and his climbing partner assisted at an avalanche site where several people had perished. In racing down the treacherous Linda to raise the alarm, Phil's climbing partner fell into a crevasse, dragging him in also, breaking his femur (thigh bone) and arm. It took two days for Phil to be rescued from the crevasse, two days of minimal clothing (he'd left all his 'spare' clothes with the survivors of the avalanche) and 30 cm of fresh snow. Experience like that, combined with his climbing ability, were just the skills we were looking for.

As with all new team members, I was keen to do a climb with Phil before the summer rescue season started. It's by far the best way to get to know each other — and when you need to jump out of a helicopter in extreme conditions, it's essential that you know exactly how your team mates will react. The essence is to know how they climb, to have complete faith in them and their competence. In that respect, climbing, and especially extreme rescue situations, are the ultimate team sport — no room for error, no room for 'not quite', no room for excuses.

What better way than to climb Aoraki/Mount Cook.

In our case the classic New Zealand alpine ice climb, the majestic East Ridge, a grade 4 ice climb, serious but not extreme. The East Ridge is a soaring, scalloped ice ridge dividing the East and Caroline Faces of Mount Cook. The climb from the Grand Plateau involves accessing the ridge with pretty straightforward climbing on moderately steep snow slopes, skirting crevasses beneath the East Face and dealing with some bergschrunds. Once up on the arête (an arête is the term used for a mountain ridge or part of one that has the classical knife edge, almost impossible to balance on) it's front pointing for about 12 pitches (700 metres) or so of frequently hard ice, summiting just below the Middle Peak at about 3600 metres.

Like all good ideas, this one was hatched over a beer in the tavern, and the details finalised at a barbecue (more beer, we used to consider it a valuable sports food). I think at the time we also made a deal to meet Mark Whetu on the summit in two days' time — well, I waited two weeks and he still hadn't turned up, wimp. (Mark is a ski and mountain guide who was to come with me as my mountain cameraman on my return to Aoraki/Mt Cook.)

With Phil and I due to be in the hills for three or four days, Anne took baby Lucy to Christchurch to visit her mum and dad. A bit of fussing and attention from grandparents sure beats sitting around home with a lively 10-month-old, especially while I'm playing in the hills.

Never being one to expend unnecessary energy, we flew into the Grand Plateau by ski-plane on the afternoon of the 15th of November. Fantastic flight, really committing for the pilot as once on the final descent there is little chance of pulling out or turning back, the only option is to land. The change from a bustling airport full of tourists to the incredible stillness of the plateau, tucked in under Tasman, has to be experienced. As soon as the ski-plane takes off leaving you behind, you feel a real commitment to the task ahead, a real excitement about being in that elemental place.

We roped up and wove through the partially hidden crevasses to the hut, perched on the rim of the plateau, overlooking the Hochstetter Ice Fall. On the way over, our eyes were constantly drawn to the East Ridge, standing out in profile in front of us. Decision time at the hut, climb from there at midnight or make use of the afternoon light to do the route-finding across the plateau and up the broad shelf under the East Face, then bivvy for a few hours ('bivvy' is the shortened term for 'bivouac', meaning to camp out, preferably under the stars, generally without a tent but using any helpful natural features for protection, such as rock outcrops and overhangs or crevasses). After sorting through our gear, hurriedly packed that morning, we decided on the bivvy idea. We cooked a meal at the Plateau Hut, cutting down on the food to carry.

I climb light, always have and still do. I guess there are two ways of looking at it: if you carry everything for every eventuality then you invariably have to use it, as heavy loads slow you down; or go light, just enough for survival, not comfort, and climb quick.

That evening we trudged across the Grand Plateau in soft snow, down from the hut and across the kilometre to the shelf under the East Face. Constantly on the alert for avalanches off the face, although we had waited until the sun had gone off it to minimise the danger. At the

Plateau Hut and the east face of Aoraki. The Linda Glacier is the river of broken ice on the right of the photo.

base of the ridge we found a safe spot in a large crevasse, or bergschrund, and settled down for a few hours of darkness.

That was when I realised all the things I had forgotten, number one of which was my closed-cell sleeping pad to keep my butt off the snow. Insulation from the snow is critical, as most clothing relies on air trapped between fibres and layers, and when you compress all the air out with your weight through your butt, the cold sucks the heat out of you rapidly. Sleeping mats are made with closed-cell foam, so the air is trapped in, cushioning and, more importantly, insulating your body from the ice. I spent a few uncomfortable hours sitting on the rope thinking I'm glad I don't have to do this for long — little did I know. We carried snack food, enough for breakfast and the climb, knowing that there would be a huge cook-up back at Plateau Hut the next night. The thing we probably regretted that night was no Primus stove, the little portable gas burner. We had plenty of fluids, both from snow melt on the rocks and what we had carried, but a hot coffee would have gone down a treat.

At 5 am, after a damp night spent with our feet in our packs, what freeze there was had settled, so we headed up. The freeze in alpine ice and snow climbing is critical, the ideal conditions are always those where you stay on top of the snow pack, rather than wallowing through it. A good freeze also binds up a lot of the unstable ice and rocks above, meaning, in most cases, less danger of being hit. The exception is when melt from the previous day freezes and expands (as anyone who has frozen a bottle of any liquid in the freezer will know, when fluids freeze they expand with great force, and will break the bottle or pop the top). In the mountains this generally happens in the early morning, 5 am or so, giving rise to some ice and rock falls. No chance of that happening this particular morning, it looked clear and above us were the steep, partially frozen snow slopes to the crest of the East Ridge. The snow was soft and energy sapping, more of a trudge than anything. I led and Phil carried the rope, probably the last time he would let a lightweight like me get away with that, as being heavier he was continually punching deeper than my tracks, both of us struggling in the frustrating conditions.

On cresting the ridge at the level but knife-sharp arête about a third of the way up, the exposure between your legs is awesome. The steep ice ridge soars up to Middle Peak in a scalloped arête and swoops down the Caroline Face to the ice rubble at its base thousands of feet below. Unfortunately for us the ice wasn't the clean cramponing we had expected and hoped for, but dinner-plates of blue ice. That meant fixed belays and careful moving. Mares' tails had started to form over the summit ridge, which meant there were extremely high winds up there, though we were still in the lee of the winds and in relatively calm conditions. The climbing was painstakingly slow, pitch after pitch of hard ice, and chopping out stances for belays and placing icescrews took valuable time. I was grateful for my weird-looking MacInnes Pterodactyl ice hammer as the more traditionally shaped Chouniard ice axe kept bouncing back out or was shearing off large plates of ice.

The weather was building all this time, wind increasing in intensity and mares' tails turning into the beginnings of hogs' backs. But climb on we did, in the confidence of youth. Or perhaps it was the lack of a decision to go back? I was once told that the difference between giving up and showing real guts is just the lack of a decision to stop. As long as you think, 'I'll just go on another 10 metres, another 100 metres, should I stop?', as long as you can't make up your mind, it's OK.

Two things were paramount in my mind and subsequent decision making in those last four or five pitches. First, Phil was getting tired, I led those last pitches to speed everything up so going back down the East Ridge in those conditions (bad ice, storm building) wasn't going to be on as neither of us had the strength or equipment to downclimb in such poor conditions. The exposed East Ridge is not a place to be in a storm. Second, Phil was a big strong guy compared to me with my puny frame, so I knew he'd be able to handle the wind at the top, and it's only a few pitches down off Middle Peak (just a wander on a nice day) to Porter Col — three abseils and we would be on the Upper Empress Shelf, virtually home free.

Cresting the summit ridge of Cook was quite a shock; we were tired, not necessarily thinking that well, and it was blowing like a bastard. Have you ever experienced a truly fierce wind, one that howls and hammers at you? One that beats your face with your helmet strap until it's red raw, flaps your jacket hood, blows your ice screws and slings around, and, even worse, picks you up off your ice axe, ice hammer and crampons and moves you towards a 1700-metre drop.

Don't.

It's the scariest thing in the world. The wind in that environment can have an evil life force of its own, sucking your energy out of you by making you fight it and the wind chill it freezes you with.

It was 6 pm on the 16th of November and we were in the teeth of a south-westerly jet stream. I lowered Phil down from the Middle Peak, and froze almost solid doing it, almost paralysed. I scampered down to Phil, stuffed around with the rope, continually getting tangled in the wind, that bloody wind. We had to yell, almost scream to be heard, even up close. On down, need shelter. The one thing I knew was that the wind was killing us; we weren't quite as invincible as I'd thought.

Run, fly, float to the nearest 'schrund, and a miserable hole it was too. What happened to the textbook cavern that's supposed to be in every bergschrund when needed?

Welcome to Middle Peak Hotel.

Time to take stock of our situation.

Clothing: woollen vest next to my skin, cotton glacier shirt, just in case the sun came out, pile jacket and Gore-Tex shell. The bottom half was pile pants and Gore-Tex salopettes. On my feet were some of my Granny's natural wool socks in my new Raichle plastic alpine boots plus two pairs of dry socks. We both had balaclava-style hats and Phil had an extra couple of wool layers and a cosy-looking down duvet.

Food: about half a packet of Shewsburys left from the climb, a wee tin of peaches, a couple of packets of drink mixture and a Moro bar for emergencies. A drink bottle each, almost empty after the climb.

Phil had a closed-cell foam mat, while I sat on the rope and any other gear I could find. Other than that we didn't have much else. Not that it mattered as we were only going to be in the slot a night or two at the most.

Priority number one was some shelter from the wind funnelling through the tunnel. No options on the hill side, just pure blue ice, hard as marble. On the bridge side (outside wall of the tunnel) there was an alcove that looked the only option. After some work it was a three-sided hole with a partial wall of sugary snow and ice blocks, not the most inviting but a damn sight better than the alternative outside. The hole wasn't quite big enough to stretch out in, not quite big enough to sit right up in and had a bit of a curve in it. Spindrift kept floating in, but was manageable. It was cold from the outset, probably -5 to -10°C lowering to below -20°C at times.

A thought about the weather: What we were expecting was a traditional four- or five-day cycle of increasing north-westerly winds, reaching a peak as a cold front moved up the South Island, followed by a southerly flow, bringing cold temperatures, some snow and clearing weather. But unfortunately a very unusual set of circumstances was to develop.

My friend Bob Munro describes those weather patterns in an extract from the *New Zealand Alpine Club Journal* of 1983:

> The Southern Oscillation index, a measurement of the relative strengths between two of the Pacific's most important weather balancing acts — the Australian-Indonesian low and the high-pressure system east of Tahiti — had begun one of its periodic shifts. Pressures rose in the centre of the low system bringing widespread drought in Australia, while the Central Eastern Pacific experienced devastating cyclones. The phenomenon 'El Niño' affected most continents that year except Europe. The normally positioned Pacific high decayed until the pressure imbalance between Tahiti and Darwin was the strongest ever. In New Zealand this meant the establishment of a strong south-west jet stream in the upper air layers showed unusual persistence.

That first night was really a template for the other 12 to follow. While we had every confidence we would be able to climb out in sunshine in the morning, training took over. For a start we rationed the little food we had from day one, one biscuit each in the morning, as much water as we could melt (about half a cup each) and a few grams of drink powder. We put dry socks on and kept our boots on too, to keep both the boots and the feet warm and supple, ready to climb out in the morning, and then climbed into our packs for the first night (our packs had extensions to them that meant they could be used like a short bivvy bag coming up to our thighs for a bit of extra protection).

Morning brought all bad news, still blowing a gale, wind sounding like a freight train. The morning ritual was gear up, boots laced up, crampons and rope on, and outside for a look. That first morning, the 17th of November, we started out, all geared up and ready to forge through the wind down to Porter Col and beyond. About 10 metres was enough to know it was even worse than before, so we crawled back up and into the hole again. Managed only to freeze ourselves to the bone.

So, back into the alcove, loosen the boots, feet freezing. Sweat from the liners had soaked the dry socks and even at the end of that first day I knew we would end up with some frostbite.

Much of the time was spent lying as still as possible, constantly monitoring each other, trying to keep feet warm with some massage and elevation, trying to keep the spindrift that continually blew in off our bodies. We needed to ensure that the boots were still fitting well, so we'd be ready to climb out as soon as the wind abated.

We spent five days in that routine, monitoring the food, restricting ourselves to one biscuit and some drink mix daily and, most importantly, trying to melt some water. I had the Moro bar up on the wall for that real emergency. The up-side of eating only a few hundred calories a day and burning thousands, of drinking only 100 mls of fluid but losing 100s of mls was that you didn't have to worry about baring the body to take a leak or a dump. This is reflected in the old saying, 'If you don't eat, you don't shit . . .'; unfortunately the same saying goes on to state '. . . if you don't shit, you die.'

Our feet became a real worry on the Thursday (Day 3 on Middle Peak). My big toes had frozen and my feet had started to swell, classic first steps of serious frostbite. The attempt to get out on the Friday was pretty half hearted as technical climbing with numb feet wasn't going to be easy.

By Saturday (20th November) we knew that we were only going to get out with outside help. Feet had swollen so the plastic boot shells wouldn't fit over the liners, and the toes on both my feet had become white and waxy looking, just like in all the textbooks.

It was like your own little Discovery Channel playing at the end of your legs. All I could think was, 'Yep, it really is as solid as a piece of frozen steak, just like we were taught.'

Continually I would wonder about what was happening down below — as each day ticked by, I would think, 'Well, today they'll be doing this or that, and they'll be expecting me to do this or that also.' A unique situation really, understanding that your job, especially from day four or five, is to stay alive so they won't waste their time and effort when the weather finally clears. On about day four, when I knew it was unlikely that we were ever going to get out under our own steam, I hung my helmet, some slings and climbing gear on an ice screw outside — stuff that would flap around in the wind and stay free of snow and ice build-up, so if there was a clearance it would be seen by helicopter or telescope from the village.

By Sunday, the sixth day, we had given ourselves anywhere from 36 to 48 hours to live. Food was almost gone, we were weak and I was going downhill fast. With no body fat, a scrawny 59 kilos, I was catabolising a lot of muscle to survive. In fact I came out of there at under 46 kilos, losing over 13 kilos in 14 days — not many diets can beat that.

I was desperately concerned that someone would get hurt in trying to rescue us. I knew that it would be difficult for my friends below to stay detached and professional, as it's when you get even slightly distracted from the job at hand that mistakes occur in the mountains.

Phil and I were in total isolation during these days, not just in a cramped cold hole but also mentally. I probably pissed Phil off regularly by wanting to talk all the time. I've always looked upon any silence as a bit of a challenge; Phil quite the opposite. Where I would be happy to chat about my family all day he wasn't keen to talk much about his at all. Frustrating for me, annoying for him, but no getting away from each other so just a matter of making a compromise.

We were blissfully and thankfully unaware of what was happening in the village below, things that we only found out after the ordeal was over.

The following is how Bob Munro describes that time:

> By Thursday evening (Day 3) we were getting really concerned. Although it was raining and blowing in the village climbers had managed to move down from Gardiner. If it had been at all possible to move high on the mountain since the strong winds had developed on Monday, then this was the day.
>
> A fixed wing overflight was planned for the next day. However, on Friday morning the weather forecast predicted continuing gale force winds. Realising that Mark and Phil didn't have sleeping bags or a stove we moved into full search and rescue 'standby'. The pattern that was to become so

familiar over the next week and a half was established that day. Getting geared up. Doing the mental exercise to shift mind ahead to whatever situation the body might be whisked away to in this age of rapid helicopter transport. Then sitting there, and sitting there — like the runner being called to the blocks but never getting the release of the gun. The nervous tension builds up but is never channelled into action.

The weather worsened throughout Saturday and Sunday. Snow fell to low levels and the Ball Hut road was closed because of avalanche danger. The anemometer was ripped off its bolts at Tasman Saddle. Yet there was just the hint in the forecasts that the wind could slacken during the brief lulls between the rapidly advancing fronts. Ron Small had a close call with some cloud that developed around his helicopter during a recce of the lower East Ridge. By Sunday night Tony Teeling and Peter Brailsford were established in Plateau Hut and confirmed Mark and Phil's plans from the intentions book. The establishment of the widespread weather-watch and build-up of medical equipment had begun. Gary Rees constructed another of his boil-the-billy-warm-air-revival contraptions, and plans were made to fly in Dr Dick Price when Mark and Phil were found. The daily routine involved a flurry of pre-dawn activity followed by tense waiting through first-light, which often offered the best chance of a respite from the wind and cloud. Then the gradual dispersal of people to different jobs. Ringing relatives, revising yet again the well-worn options, trying to keep the rest of the place functioning, and dealing with the growing press corps.

Monday 22nd (Day 7). The cloud base had lifted a little and just after 9 am Ron Small flew four climbers up the Hooker hoping to land them on the white-ice from where they could struggle up to Gardiner. He actually touched down on bare ice above the hut and as everybody clambered out his forward speed indicator registered 80 knots! Helicopters have been taking the drudgery and hard work out of alpine rescue for some time now. The Squirrel was showing that it could function at the edge of climbable conditions.

I remember the day being particularly difficult. During the twice daily phone calls to relatives it was becoming harder to press an optimistic outlook. It seemed important to a lot of people to have a view on whether they were alive or not. Chief Ranger Bert Youngman was among the few who seemed to have single-minded confidence in the outcome. Yet the evidence was so skimpy. Most of the research work has been done on victims of immersion hypothermia. Other overstayers at altitude on Mount Cook had sleeping bags and stoves at least for part of their isolation. I rang Dr Dick Price and read out the estimated minimum temperatures they would have experienced, given that the only hope of them being alive was the 'schrund below the Middle Peak. I asked him to put a limit on their survival. I felt sorry to put pressure on him but he seemed the only one who could give a much-needed answer. He thought that 10 days after they had finished their food was about the limit. So, if they had two days' food that would put the cut-off at day 12 — Saturday, four more days. OK, we'll go with that for a while.

Right now it was important to get some sleep into the system. The dairy-farmer starts were beginning to tell. I made a quick trip to Twizel for some knockout pills to make the maximum use of the night-time hours. Coming back along Highway 80 the mountain decided to reveal itself! Great orographic clouds were swirling around in the Hooker and others were streaming out over the East Face, however, the whole of the summit ridge was visible! By the time I got back to the village Gardiner was reporting daylight above them and Ron Small was on his way in yet again.

So far we had spent about 156 hours or 9360 minutes on Middle Peak, with no sleeping bags or Primus to warm and feed us. Middle Peak had become our existence, the wind our continual tormentor, the cold a constant nagging dull ache. I only remember shivering uncontrollably a few times, the rest of those 9000 minutes being continually aware of the cold, the discomfort, the hunger, the thirst.

The nights were always the worst; for some reason it's easy to nap during the day but hard to sleep at night. Also, the feeling of being totally isolated is magnified at night in the dark, the other one asleep, just your thoughts to keep you company. I continually and increasingly felt a frustration at not being able to move about. I dreamt of sparkling clear water. I pictured every page of my favourite recipe books, promising myself to make all the classics and savour every one of them as soon as I got down, and promising myself I would have a glass of cold clear water every morning for the rest of my life. I was also starting to feel claustrophobic, just mildly, but being trapped there with no options played on my mind.

External stimuli were minimal and very negative (howling wind and bone-seeping cold) so every thought and action had to come from inside yourself, difficult day after day, hour after hour and, even worse, minute after minute.

Phil was always there, stoic in his strength, but not the world's best conversationalist as I have said. We were focused, we had a job to do, and that was to survive.

2 MIDDLE PEAK HOTEL: CHECKING OUT

SEARCH LOG, Monday 22 November, Day 7

1914 hrs HWW (Hotel Whiskey Whiskey, call sign of Ron Small's helicopter) — have located one climber, red jacket waving from 'schrund to north-west of Porter Col.

1922 hrs Dr Dick Price on way to Mount Cook.

1932 hrs HWW — have lost drop bag. Request from Don Bogie to prepare climbing team to drop on lower Empress Shelf.

1935 hrs HWW returns to Park Headquarters.

1940 hrs Decision made to continue throwing out drop kits and then place four climbers on lower Empress Shelf.

2025 hrs Successful first drop, second and third.

2049 hrs Radio call: 'This is Hotel Middle Peak. Mark lost feeling in all toes, no food since Wednesday. Phil, two big toes frozen, 'sched' in 30 minutes.'

We'd been listening to the varying intensity of the wind (from freight train to jet engine howl) for seven long days. Now the wind was still howling, but the beat of Hotel Whiskey Whiskey's blades sounded through it like magic. After seven days of isolation and hope, we were in a panic to respond, to get ready to be rescued and leave Middle Peak Hotel, that icy cold and cramped hole. Fumbling with frozen feet and fingers was a frustrating nightmare. We were weak from having no food, but the sound of the helicopter was unmistakeable and the ultimate motivation, not the time to be caught out by being unprepared or late. But once we felt the force of the wind, the fact that there was to be no immediate rescue was instantly apparent — no going home today.

I was too weak to help, seven days of using my body heat to melt snow and no food had wiped me out. Phil was out at the 'schrund mouth (I'm not even sure if he was on the rope) waving at the helicopter. There was no room to move in the 'doorway' of the hole, no room to move outside with the steep slope leading to a drop of 300 metres down over ice cliffs to the Empress Shelf.

The first bag teetered on the edge of the hole, then bounced down away out of reach and the chopper disappeared down the valley. Waiting for it to come back, if it was to come back, was hell. A combination of elation that they knew where to look, that they'd found us, and a huge concern that they would push the limits too far with someone getting hurt. Almost an hour went by, during which time we tried to make ourselves ready for escape in case the wind dropped or a head appeared in the doorway of our hole.

To our relief the chopper did come back, and with Phil on the rope, belayed out at the entrance of our hole, everything started to happen fast.

Phil dragged the first bag in and then ducked straight back out to grab another as Ron went windmilling past again. Three passes, three bags, with the last bag landing right on Phil. Then silence, just the howling wind, gathering darkness and back into our hole.

It was like Christmas: sleeping bags, bivvy booties and thermoses of hot fluids. A Primus stove, cans of food, chocolate and radios spelt survival, spelt rescue.

That first contact with Park Headquarters was a time of elation — we'd received the essentials for survival just in time. We went from operating on a grim determination to survive, depending on the knowledge that they knew us, that they would have faith in our strength, to almost passing over the responsibility for our survival to those on the other end of the radio waves.

Food and fluids were a real priority, downing some chocolate and warm drink first, followed by a can of Irish stew, I think. We didn't even wait for it to warm up, just wolfed it down.

From then on the radio became an extension of my arm, my fingers, became to some degree my strength. We worked out rapidly how best to communicate using a system that involved one or two presses of the transmit button so as to conserve the batteries. Questions were relayed to us in a yes or no form, their understanding of our situation becoming apparent with every well thought-out question. Listening in at sched time was relatively frugal on batteries but transmitting was very hungry on power. The cold reduced battery life dramatically, making performance of the radios even worse. And apart from anything else, dropping radios from helicopters doesn't do them much good at all.

It was fantastic to hear familiar voices over the radio, to hear the competence and confidence in their voices. The rescue headquarters at the park had obviously been in touch with our families on a regular basis. Those first seven days must have been especially hard for them and for Anne, with all of us so intimately involved in village life.

The rest of the night was spent organising our haul of goodies, getting dry, warm clothing and sleeping bags sorted, and bivvy booties on our feet.

Day 8, Tuesday, the 23rd of November, brought the wind back with a vengeance, temperatures dropped even lower. A decision was made by someone to perk us up by having messages from relatives relayed to us, to have Anne talk to me on the radio. It was a stilted, brief conversation which I remember very little of, sort of:

'Sorry about this, Anne, don't worry, we're fine, be out of here soon, miss you.'

'Glad you're OK, hang in there, love you.'

All I could envisage was Anne sitting in the Search and Rescue room in the basement of Park Headquarters with a whole bunch of people, some friends, some strangers, Lucy in her arms, and Anne trying to express herself in that strange, stressful environment. It was the worst idea — I was at once elated, nervous, gutted, impatient, everything. I wanted to get out then and there, and, in fact, at times over the next six days and long nights I even tried. It almost destroyed my focus, my

Bob Munro, Anne and Lucy (10 months) at a press interview, November 1982 at Park Headquarters.

single-minded determination to show my professionalism and to survive no matter what.

I'm sure there is probably a written record in a radio log somewhere of our conversation, but I can't imagine why anyone would want to dredge it up unless it was to show others in a similar situation what not to do.

Those last six days in Middle Peak Hotel will always be a hazy kaleidoscope of emotions and memories for me. Frequently I can't get the timing of events right, the time being a real mix of elation and devastation. Much of my time was spent in a dream world — actually, much nearer a nightmare world at times.

It has taken me years to confront the recurring nightmare of being so weak and ill that I hallucinated, the realisation that I am not invincible. It will always be difficult for me to differentiate between what was dream and what was reality in that time, in much the same way that it is almost impossible to differentiate between an amputee's 'phantom' pain and 'real' pain.

The most powerful dream or image I have from those last days was that I was in a hilly city suburb, barefoot in a snow storm. All I had to do was walk down a slope and then up an icy sidewalk, beside a snow-covered road. I could feel my frozen, frostbitten feet stumbling in the dark but I continued on. The houses along the road were all in darkness, no one responding to my hammering at their doors. The end, the escape, was just ahead near the top of the hill.

The scary thing is that in reality, in my delirious state, I really did try to get up and go out, to go home, and probably would have if Phil hadn't bounced me back into some semblance of reality.

Days 8, 9 and 10 merged together, a continuum of blowing snow, howling gales and a return to rationing food, fluids and fuel. We attached the empty drop bags outside to flap around in the hurricane-strength breeze, just as I had done on the third day with my climbing gear.

Nights were still terrible, hours of waiting, waiting and thinking. When rescued I had frostbite to several fingers from continually pressing the light button on my watch. The VHF radio died after three days or so, the battery flat. Probably it could have gone on for a day more, but I was always turning it on, every hour on the hour, desperate for news of the weather abating and an imminent rescue.

By Day 12 (Saturday, the 27th of November) a chest infection I had developed was worsening. Lying down in our little hole in my severely weakened condition was getting too much. I was still constantly visualising my cookbooks, page by page, recipe by recipe. I would desperately try to picture Anne's face, Lucy's face, Mum's and Dad's. I'd almost panic when I couldn't, only to feel relief late at night when they would suddenly come to me.

Actually, we realised that we had the easy part of the job in hand: to survive, to manage our bodies and minds as best as we could. The rescue staff and our families had the hard job: the critical decision-making affecting not just our lives but those of all who were attempting to rescue us; the dealing with the media; and the pressure from so many uninformed or poorly informed people to do something, anything. I know Ron has always said that a lot of the missions flown were just done so as to be seen to be doing something rather than for any concrete, positive reason.

Day 13, Sunday, the 28th of November, our last full day in the 'schrund, not that we knew that. For us it was just lying there, totally dependent on rescue now as we had been for the last nine days, the hour and minutes interminably slow. That evening the skies started to clear, the wind dropped and helicopter activity was starting again.

Lying there in Middle Peak Hotel, just before dusk I jerked upright, 'Phil can you hear that?'

The sound of a chopper — an Iroquois I thought — you could hear the distinctive 'whop whop whop' of its huge blades. Then a huge bang, a loud (to me anyway) slapping noise.

'Shit, I think it's crashed!'

I'll never know whether I actually heard it or felt it or what, but I sure knew something bad had happened. I couldn't think of anything other than the possibility that someone had been killed. Later, just before dark, HWW appeared with another drop bag. More food, some gear, a

Iroquois 03 on her back on the Empress Shelf, 28th November 1982.

VHF radio that didn't survive the fall and a transistor radio, which was crucial.

Lying there in the dark, we listened to Radio Scenicland I think, 3ZA. We heard that a rescue was planned for the morning — no sleep that night.

Monday, the 29th of November, was the birthday of Kevin Hathaway (my father-in-law, Anne's dad), and for us it was Day 14 in Middle Peak Hotel.

Dawn brought clearing skies, wisps of southerly mist wafting up over the Caroline. Phil was out at the 'door' watching and waiting, me back inside, not much use for anything. The morning report on breakfast radio tells of a wrecked Iroquois lying 600 metres below us on the Empress Shelf. Shit, it was true! Christ, who's been hurt? Thoughts tumbled through our minds, thoughts of friends, and desperate hope that they are OK.

Bert Youngman, Chief Ranger at Mount Cook, is on the next radio news at 7.30 am describing, I'm sure for our benefit, the rescue plans for today. We 'spring' into action, or at least Phil does. It's finally time to go home. Phil and I are pensive, wondering who will be on the strop, has to be Don. A mixture of worry, anticipation, this is it.

Bob Munro describes those days from his perspective at the base, immersed in the events for two weeks at Park Headquarters:

> By now all New Zealand was following the drama via their TV sets and radio news bulletins. But there was so little to report. After two more days, radio contact was lost with the pair. Although it was probably just battery failure, the lack of contact increased the anxiety.
>
> By Friday 26 November, four days after they had been found and 11 days since they started climbing, a partial respite on the lower slopes of the mountain allowed the climbing team at Gardiner Hut to be brought out, but that was all. Saturday the 27th was a repeat of all the other days, but the forecast was for the south-west jet stream to weaken finally on Monday and be completely clear of the region by Tuesday. Dr Price gave two to four days' grace before any serious medical problems would develop.
>
> The next day Bert Youngman decided to bring in an RNZAF Iroquois helicopter to help in ferrying climbers, as the option of having to do a long stretcher lower was a real possibility. It arrived just after 6 pm, when the weather began another one of those 'race against the dark' evening clearances. The sky was still threatening to the south but the area around the top of Mount Cook began to clear back. So it was decided to establish a group of strong climbers on the Empress Shelf, a snow plateau about 450 metres (1500 feet) below the stranded pair. If the rescue couldn't be effected that night at least rescuers would be able to get up to the pair even in difficult conditions the next day.
>
> Events over the next hour moved swiftly.
>
> Ron Small took off in the Squirrel with a load of rescue

Kim Logan (park rescue team) in Empress Shelf advance base, 28th November 1982.

personnel. He landed them in fresh knee-deep snow on the Empress Shelf and then flew up to the summit ridge. To Ron the configuration of the snow slope seemed to have changed and he thought the bergschrund had collapsed on its occupants and he could see bodies lying out on the snow. He radioed that he was coming back and could Bert Youngman come out to the helicopter to meet him. The Search Headquarters was under virtual siege at this stage by reporters who sensed that something dramatic had happened.

Just as the Squirrel swung away from whatever had happened at Middle Peak Hotel the Iroquois came in to land at the advance base on the Empress Shelf with the rest of the rescue party. As the pilot put the machine into a hover in preparation for landing, the blades blew up drifts of the new snow. The pilot lost his horizon in the swirling whiteout, the tail plane hit the ground and the helicopter flipped onto its back, the tail plane and rotor hanging over the 1000-foot drop to the lower Empress Shelf.

The park mountaineers burst out of the side of the stricken machine, followed by the Iroquois crew. Apart from some minor injuries, no one was hurt. For Ron Small, hovering above, after two weeks of dawn-to-dusk standby and some very difficult mountain flying, this was getting to be the last straw. He had to leave the mystery of the Middle Peak bergschrund and now rescue the Iroquois crew. Daylight was fading fast and a southerly front was sweeping across the Mackenzie Country. It was snowing heavily only 25 km away down the valley from Mount Cook.

To take the pressure of reporters off his back (they knew that Ron had reported something strange), Bert Youngman sent a member of his staff out the door to the press to say that despite appearances hope was not given up for the climbers. For instance, in cases of severe hypothermia even people who appeared clinically dead had been revived.

A reporter at the back of the group picked up on those words and raced off to ring his office with the dramatic news that after all the struggle the two mountaineers overdue on Mount Cook were 'clinically dead'. Even the newsreader who had to read out the bulletin on TV looked dubious as he read the words, but the mistake had been made and the news was broadcast around the country. The shaken parents and relatives tried to ring through for verification of the dreadful news but once again the phone lines to the small alpine village went into overload.

Darkness was nearly upon the scene and time had run out for a proper rescue attempt that night. Ron Small managed to make one flight back in after bringing out the Iroquois crew. Another drop bag went over the side to the entrance of the bergschrund and, unaware of all the drama the premature news of his demise was causing, a figure in a blue jacket strolled out of the cave, picked up the bag and disappeared again. The two bodies that Ron thought he had seen were empty drop bags that the conscientious pair had staked into the snow to mark their exact location.

Monday the 29th just had to be the day. The forecast at 4 am indicated the lowest wind speeds yet at 3000 metres. At dawn the team on the Empress Shelf reported that everything above them was clear. They had finally snatched some sleep at 3 am after digging snow caves most of the night. They weren't digging just a shelter for themselves, but a potential field hospital in case evacuation only got that far before becoming bogged down by the weather. Dr Price was there with a full medical kit including oxygen and a portable defibrillator.

The only problem was that everywhere on the east of the Main Divide there was a thick sheet of low cloud. It hugged the ground around the Mount Cook village and spread far out into the Mackenzie Country. The temperature at Mount Cook was 0°C and then it began to snow, fine above, atrocious below. The forecasters were predicting a break in the clouds but it wasn't appearing. The worst possible scenario was for the rescue to get underway and then for cloud to form around the machines as they were lifting people out. Ron Small had decided that after the previous night's events he needed some

Don and Phil landing on the Empress Shelf, 29th November 1982.

support from the people he knew well. Bill Black, the legendary bush pilot from the rugged Fiordland area, came through with his Squirrel and brought with him Rex Dovey, who had taught Ron how to fly.

By 7.30 am the cloud in the Hooker Valley was still holding a ceiling of 2700 metres and the decision was made to go. It was 3200 metres out over the Tasman riverbed before the two Squirrels broke into sunlight and swung back towards the Hooker. A quick recce flight lowered another radio down to the bergschrund. Soon Phil's strong voice reported that he could be lifted out on his harness but that Mark should be moved on a stretcher.

Ron landed on the shelf and the strop system, first developed by Canadian rescue teams, was set up. The helicopter takes off with the rescuer dangling 20 metres below it, which enables him to be flown into tight locations with the helicopter hovering above. The sensation of flying this way is not unpleasant. It's similar to parachuting, usually lasts longer and there is no nasty thump at the end, so long as the pilot is doing his job.

The senior mountaineer, Don Bogie, had developed this system at Mount Cook along with Ron Small. It had been in use for two seasons, but so far had been tried only with rescuers picking up bodies in dangerous locations. Now it was Bogie's opportunity to try it out on some climbers who were still very much alive.

Also, as an aid for a quick pick-up, Bogie had adapted another Canadian modification of a European compact stretcher. The Bauman bag is a large nylon bag opening its full length with a series of attachment points that join it to the bottom of the helicopter's strop. This simple bag can be carried on the rescuer's hip, quickly unpacked, the patient rolled in and attached to the strop, with the helicopter hovering above. This way the rescuer doesn't have to detach from the strop and the helicopter spends the minimum time in the hover in a dangerous location.

So, with the cloud boiling up below them, a white wall of southerly snow showers on the horizon, and the first sign of clouds already beginning to appear over the Caroline Face, just above where Mark and Phil were trapped, they set to work.

Back in Middle Peak Hotel, we could hear the Squirrels operating out over the Hooker Glacier below us. Phil could see a Squirrel standing off in the distance, but the sound of the Squirrel coming in to hover signalled time for action.

A radio comes down on a line which Phil retrieves. He first tries to call HWW (the helicopter) with no luck but then gets Park Headquarters loud and clear. Our first concern is the crash the night before — we are desperately worried about the rescue team.

Nearest thing to an angel of mercy I'll ever see: Ron Small relaxing at the Park Headquarters after the rescue.

'Is everyone from the Iroquois all right?'

Huge relief when a Canadian twang booms out, 'Everyone's OK, Phil.'

The Squirrel comes back and here, scuttling down the tunnel to me, is Don. 'Jesus, Bogie you look beautiful,' is all I can think.

With Phil's help, Don moves me out nearer the entrance; all the time the din of the Squirrel hovering above; I'm aware Don is still attached to the strop; 'Awesome flying, Ron.'

Don and Phil strap me into the Bauman bag, then it's into the icy air, the familiar elevator-like lift and then the unmistakeable feeling of dropping rapidly, spinning under the chopper. Cloud and snow flying around, hands lowering the stretcher to the snow, unclipping, seeing Don lift back up into the freezing air. Faces crowd in, I lie strapped in still, cocooned against the elements, the faces look as relieved and as happy as I feel.

Ron and HWW come back in blowing up their own snow storm. Don lands with Phil on the strop, Ron gently settles the Squirrel 20 metres away. It seems only minutes before that we were still at the mercy of the mountain and weather, and now we're safe, in competent hands. We are bundled into HWW, as familiar as my lounge at home. I'm stretched out across the back seat, Phil's up front. The warmth, the comforting vibration of the Squirrel, the familiar smell of Jet-A1, all a continuum in my mind as we lift off the Empress Shelf and head back up and over Cook.

The shock of having to circle above the Tasman, to spiral down through a narrowing gap in the clouds and to see the snow storm in the valley below, really hits home how lucky we are. We are still thinking, 'Is everyone going to get off the mountain? Christ, I hope no one is stuck up there because of us.'

Flying down the Tasman, flying low, we go from the stark hardness of ice and rock to the grey monotony of the rock-strewn moraine. The softer tan tussock appears quickly, followed by the steely green subalpine scrub — home gets closer by the second.

The approach into and the landing on the Park Headquarters' landing pad will always be etched in my mind. I'd landed there tens of times, with park work and rescues, sometimes bringing bodies back, sometimes injured climbers, sometimes just cowboying with Ron. This time no bodies, just tears in the eyes, lump in the throat, the relief to be back in the place I loved, back with the people I loved. To see Gnome (Gary Rees), Bob Munro, and all the others, to see their relief and feel mine was like a great weight lifted. I looked around for Anne and Lucy; Bob told me, 'Later, mate, they'll see you down the valley.'

Just from the number of people and cameras around we started to get an inkling of how much trouble everyone had gone to and how much stress they were all under. I couldn't believe it was snowing, it was like a winter's day instead of the start of summer.

We were carried by stretcher into the first aid room, where Gnome was waiting with his warm-air device for treating hypothermia (not needed, sorry about that, Gnome). He tried to take my pulse but couldn't find one so we decided I must be dead, either that or he needed more training. Some of the first things we asked for were a beer and a Drum (smoke), so we were gutted when Dick thought they might do us more harm than good. We were pretty desperate for something fresh so someone ducked over to the local shop, and our first food ended up being a banana Zap (milkshake) — I definitely would've gone a beer though.

Our 310 hours at Middle Peak Hotel were over, a new day was starting, a new challenge was starting. The ordeal certainly wasn't over yet, but we had the feeling that it was a case of thanks guys, but let's get this show on the road, let's get to a hospital because we want to be back for the rest of the climbing season.

MERRY CHRISTMAS 1982

11 am, 29th November 1982.

STILL IN THE FIRST AID ROOM, Dick spent time assessing our feet, warming them, cleaning and checking for damage. This is the critical stage in frostbite, the time when huge tissue damage can be done and infection can take hold. Unfortunately by this time a lot of damage had been done while we were on the mountain. The feet had frozen to a significant extent in those first seven days in Middle Peak Hotel, and then during the last seven they probably went through a series of freeze/thaw cycles as our bodies warmed up and we consciously tried to keep our feet warm to stop the freeze.

A word or two about frostbite. When your fingers or ears go numb standing at the bus stop or on the bike and sting and tingle as they warm, that's not frostbite, that's generally frostnip and it can be treated by just blowing on your hands, or by putting a warm hand on your cold ear or nose, that sort of thing. Frostbite is when, due to extreme cold, the affected body part actually freezes. This generally happens for two

The Hawkeye cartoon, so very true: the original is one of my treasured items.

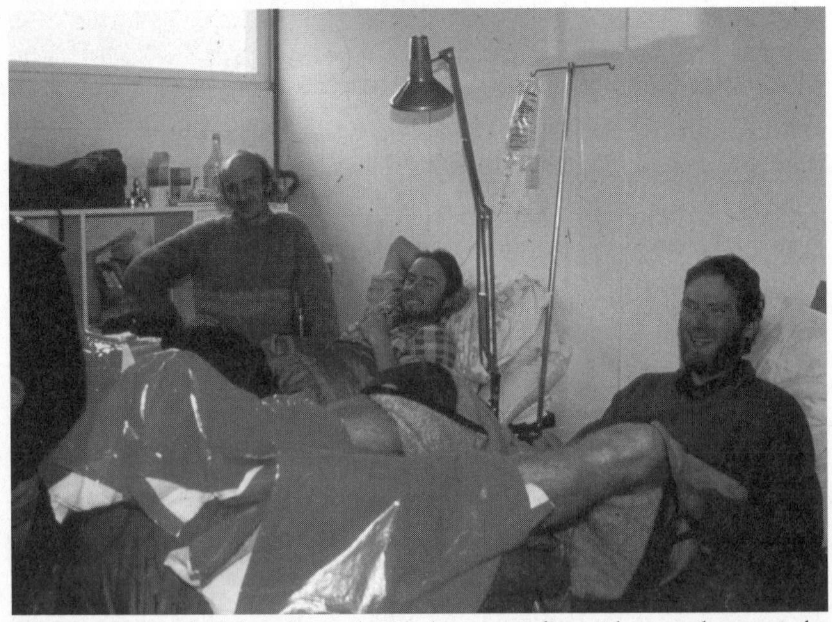

With Gnome and Phil at the Park Headquarters' first aid room: happy to be there.

reasons: one, it's bloody cold; and two, because it is so cold, your body restricts its circulation (vasoconstriction) to the extremities to maintain core body temperature. This is compounded by relatively poor circulation in your lower legs and feet. They're a long way from the heart and have a large surface area to volume ratio, which the body doesn't like when it is as bitterly cold as it is when you are fighting hypothermia.

There are several ways to classify frostbite, and a common way describes two main levels. The first is when the superficial extra-cellular fluid freezes — the stuff between the cells. This is generally near the surface, just the epidermal layers are affected, and this is frequently termed superficial or first-degree frostbite. The body can recover from this, as the actual cells that comprise our underlying tissues and vascular system are still intact and able to supply the essential elements for cell life after thawing. The more serious deep, or second-degree, frostbite is when both the inter- and intra-cellular fluid freezes — the stuff inside the cell — to a depth below the epidermis. This starts to get pretty nasty as when ice crystals form in the cells they can expand, damaging and even bursting the cells. In addition the growing crystals dehydrate the cell, cause protein denaturation, inhibition of DNA synthesis, damage to capillaries and pH changes. Simply put, that's bad news if you want the bits to recover and grow back.

Tissue injury is the greatest when the cooling is slow (that's why they snap freeze your peas), cold exposure is prolonged, and re-warming is slow. Sounds familiar doesn't it, just the conditions experienced in Middle Peak Hotel.

An even worse scenario (yes, it gets worse) is when the tissues go through freeze/thaw cycles as ours did in those last seven days. You can imitate those living conditions in the comfort of your own home to see what happens, but please, not with one of your body parts. Take a piece of meat and freeze it overnight, then take it out and leave it on the bench for the day. Freeze it again that night, and repeat for seven days — not very nice after a while. What happens is that those freeze/thaw cycles do two really bad things: they mush up or destroy the cells and leave the tissue wide open to infection during every freeze/thaw cycle.

The result is mushy rotten meat.

The reality for us was that, while some think it might have been better to leave the feet out, to let them remain frozen, the length of time we were in Middle Peak Hotel actually meant that the damage was always going to be severe, though at the time we were only aware of toes gone, not feet.

No mercy dash in the helicopter to hospital for us — because of the weather and our stable condition, we went by ambulance. Leaving Park Headquarters at Mount Cook in the old St John ambulance was really a bit of an anti-climax. I could remember the times I had been the assistant in one of our National Park ambulances, comforting people down to Twizel or Timaru. But here we were in the Twizel ambulance, heading for Burwood Hospital, Christchurch. It was a bit like packing kids up for a long trip with drinks and nibbles, treats to keep us quiet on the way. We were on stretchers, with strict instructions from Dick to keep the feet elevated and all pressure off them.

Phil and I were still somewhat confused over the fuss being made, a combination of feeling hugely relieved about being down, guilty about the trouble we had put everyone to, and anxious about our toes.

Just getting into the ambulance was a bit of a circus; greetings we had only just made to friends had to be turned into goodbyes again. I was getting to the stage where I really wanted to get going; I still hadn't seen Anne or Lucy and really wanted to get to them in Geraldine.

Down through the Mackenzie Country, heading for Mum and Dad's, propped up in the back on our stretchers, Phil and I talked of the future. Our feet didn't look too bad from this angle. We thought, 'Oh well, there go a few toes, the sooner they're gone the sooner we'll be back.' We thought of all the climbers we knew around the world without toes, and there are plenty — no problem.

As the ambulance was going through Fairlie we talked them into stopping to buy a newspaper to catch up on what was happening around the world. There we were, on the front page. We laughed at all the supposition and inaccuracies in the story, especially the diagram of Middle Peak Hotel, the ice cave. From somewhere, probably a mountaincraft manual, some well-meaning soul had reproduced a line drawing of a classic snow cave. The drawing described sleeping benches above the height of the door, cooking benches and a nicely sloped entrance way that kept the elements out. This was a Rolls Royce, a Presidential Suite of a cave. If only they knew about our cramped, blue-ice, hard, lumpy, draughty and spindrift-filled hole.

Over the hills from Fairlie to Geraldine, I felt decidedly car sick — nothing worse for someone prone to car sickness than to drive over hills lying down and facing the wrong way.

Geraldine was a pretty unique experience, ambulance up the drive, we were carted into the lounge on our stretchers and having afternoon tea and scones. This was my first chance in over two long weeks to catch up with Anne, to see the real concern on the faces of all the family. It was, in many ways though, an interlude of normality before what was going to be a marathon hospital stay.

Nothing is ever straightforward really; a simple drive from Geraldine to Christchurch turned into a tour of the city's suburbs for a while as we actually got lost trying to find Burwood Hospital. I will always remember Phil and me grabbing the map and navigating through the eastern part of the city.

The images of our arrival will always be the media, and the concerned look on the faces of the staff, faces we came to know intimately over the coming months. The entrance hasn't changed since that time, as a recent visit showed, and it looked 30 years old then. We were wheeled out of the ambulance, said our thanks to the drivers, and entered a new version of our ice cave — the confines of Burwood Hospital's Ward 7, the 'plastics' ward.

But before you can enter their domain, you need to check in, just like in a hotel. It was all a bit of a blur, endless questions, trying to ascertain what condition we were in mentally and physically. Always of concern were our feet, as the hospital staff tried to determine exactly what had been done and what was to be done. Of almost equal concern was our malnourishment, our general health. By the time the doors had closed we had our first Complan shakes in our hands, the first of many.

No offence to Complan, but I really hated them from the first mouthful. I had just spent 14 days surviving on the 'virtual' cooking of fantastic meals, promising myself the most elegant food and concentrated flavours possible and I had to scull Complan. It certainly wasn't the best introduction to my working relationship with the dietitian.

With Anne at my side and my family close at hand I had the support I needed to carry on. Hospital became a continuous series of tests, of treatments, of boredom; the start of a time of growing pain and frustration.

Pretty much right from the start they had Phil and me in separate rooms, isolated for three reasons I guess: to protect us from the continual attention; for sterility; and by our own choice. There was plenty of unwanted attention from the media, the public, and people who believed we needed their help in some weird and wonderful ways, when to a certain degree we really just wanted to be left alone. We were in virtual isolation anyway, to minimise the otherwise high risk of infection, but I think everyone could tell, especially if they had consulted my friends at Mount Cook, that two weeks isolated together in Middle Peak Hotel was more than enough for both of us. By the time we hit hospital and the requirement to just survive had gone, it was time to go back to our own worlds. We didn't start out as close friends, in fact that whole climb was to investigate each other — certainly had the opportunity to do that. I think in the weeks stuck in hospital our character differences became quite clear: Phil strong, firm of opinion, pretty stoic really; me as bright as can be, bit of a court jester at times.

With frostbite the treatments available are somewhat limited, and much of the time was focused on analysing how deep the damage went and how far up the leg. We had thermal imaging and radio imaging to determine what was still vascularised, that is, what still had a flow of oxygen and nutrients being delivered by our blood supply.

It was those studies that really hit home the seriousness of what we were facing. Stewart Sinclair, our surgeon at that time, indicated that it was likely that all our toes and at least part of the feet would be lost.

For me, and I'm sure it was planned that way by our medical team, the concept of losing more than a few toes, losing the whole limb, was a gradual process or at least a series of incremental steps. The idea was for us to come to terms with the necessity of it all, to come to terms with the scale of the problem. My first thought was, as always, get another opinion. I felt bad in some ways, felt I was denigrating Stewart, but I desperately wanted Dick Price's opinion. As an expedition doctor and mountain medicine specialist, Dick had dealt with frostbite, dealt with all the things going on with us in many different circumstances.

It was really only after working in medicine after my degree studies that I actually understood how much research and advice someone like Stewart Sinclair seeks in these rare situations. Dick didn't need to say much though, one look at his face after a visit was enough for me to see that this was really going to happen, things were very bad and we had little in the way of choice or say in the matter.

For the staff, one of the problems with having Phil and me in hospital was that for a lot of the time we probably weren't sick enough, so we tended to stick our noses into everything and had an opinion about everything. Dr Inglis and Dr Doole was the common term I believe, and probably not used all that affectionately at times. From the first minutes in hospital, I always wanted to know what the medical team were doing and why. Having done so much basic and advanced first aid at Mount Cook for so many years, I understood most of the things happening to me and was pretty intolerant of staff learning on me. If I was getting a drug I wanted to know what drug it was, what it did, and what the complications might be. If it was an IV line, where were they going to put it, how often were they going to clear any blockages and with what. I was so full of questions and opinions I must have been a real pain in the arse to professionals who just wanted to get on with their jobs, but it was my body, even if it was in a poor state of repair.

The IV lines (intravenous lines, needles or plastic tubes inserted into a vein in your arm or hand to administer fluids or drugs directly to your blood stream) were always a problem. The larger plastic tubes always seemed to block — even when they tried to keep the sites free with heparin solutions and the like, my body just wanted to clot them up. I must admit I really didn't like the technique some nurses had for clearing the lines, in fact late one night I went off my nut at one poor nurse doing it. The technique involved winding the IV tube tightly around a ballpoint pen and pulling hard on the other end. By tugging on the line the tube was pulled around the tight bends or wraps, forcing the fluid in the tube between the pen and my arm into my vein, clearing any obstruction and getting fluids flowing. The only problem was it felt like a hot poker going up my arm and that I did not like. After a few attempts they resorted to mostly using the small butterfly needles, generally in veins in the back of my hand. These seemed to stay clear for longer although the veins broke down more often and hence they had to be shifted more regularly. Give me an extra needle any day rather than the ballpoint trick, thanks.

I never realised how much repetition was on the radio until all those weeks lying there. Television didn't interest me much and I have a thirst for information, so to hear the same news or songs repeated tens of times a day was hellishly boring. Books have always been important to me, never more so than in those weeks. I read books by amputees (Sir Douglas Bader of course, and Norman Croucher, a double amputee climber from the UK, about 10 years older than me), books on climbing and on my other obsession during those years, aviation. In fact I probably worried more about not being able to finish my private pilot's licence than I did about climbing, as flying was my newest passion.

I flew so much in my job at the park that it was impossible not to catch the flying bug. Every winter there were hours in ski-planes on the Tasman Glacier and in helicopters, heli-skiing. The summer was dominated by helicopters for rescue and park work such as track and hut maintenance. Every minute of flying I was constantly scanning the gauges, checking on all the hand movements of the pilot, filing all the images away for when I could fly myself. Aviation books and magazines, not just on how to fly, but technical theory, operations text and stories of marathon or extreme flights, filled in many days with both reading and dreaming.

The trouble with any brain power thing in those weeks was that it involved a battle against pain and the side effects of pain relief. As the feet progressively rotted, as the gangrene set in, so did the pain. Pain relief came in the form of codeine-based pills, stronger with the passing weeks. The problem with them and with the morphine-based pain management after the amputations is that they take your momentum away with the pain. They also make your eyes tired, meaning that even reading the simplest of books can be too much at times.

Anne was in every day, some days with Lucy (which wasn't always easy), and on many days several times. Mum and Dad travelled up from Geraldine, 150 km each way, every second or third day. They all became the nucleus of my hospital life.

I found that the people involved in your hospital life when you're there a long time fall into three categories. First there are the nurses, doctors, orderlies and other staff who control your day. These are the people you spend your entire time around, days and nights, they become your hospital family in lots of ways. Anne and Lucy belonged in that group as well, being with me for so many hours a day and through so many of the procedures. Lucy was almost adopted by the staff at Burwood, learning to walk in the corridors, frequently beside my wheelchair. Then there are the regular visitors, people like Mum and Dad, close family and friends. With these people, if you are having a bad day you can just lie there, if you are having a good day they're fun. They are people who you want to have around. The last group are the visitors who are just hard work. It's amazing how short even a saint's temper and concentration span can get in a situation like that, let alone how Phil and I coped. You just want to tell some people to 'bugger off', as both Phil and I did occasionally. Phil was definitely better at it than me though.

Visiting time seems to be the focus of hospital life, to have everyone washed and treated, sitting up in bed waiting for the visitors. On many days, apart from the visits from close family and friends who were all devious enough to sneak in at all hours, the visit time was a real trial. Many people were just too hard, you really didn't want to see them, let alone be nice to them. But on the side were the surprises, like a group of

Taranaki climbers, bowling in larger than life, taking everyone in the ward by storm. Smuggling in whiskey (good for the circulation apparently) and taking us for a spin in the chairs, real breaths of fresh mountain air. After visiting hours were up there was either a sense of relief or sometimes a feeling of real depression, the old urge to get the hell out of there.

The morning mailbag was always a delight. It was rare that we missed out on mail and common to have screeds of it. I think every school kid in Canterbury and a lot of places further away did projects on us. My room was always full of primary school art, 'get well' letters and cards from far and wide. Telegrams from friends around the world, politicians and just plain strangers flooded in. Each day Anne helped sort out what needed answering straight away, and what didn't need answering at all.

In addition to that attention came the media in all its forms. For the first few days we were hidden away, as it was all just too much. But the realisation of how big a deal it had become to the whole country prompted me to convince Phil that we should do a combined press release. Get them all together, give them 10 minutes after we had said our thanks to everyone, and get it all over and done with in one hit.

I can't remember the exact day but anyway that's what we did. It was all arranged for us, TV, the papers and radio were all there down in the sunroom off the end of the ward. We were wheeled down in our beds. I was still pretty much flat on my back, but Phil was sitting up and looking good. The Burwood staff were very protective, like security guards, limiting the questions and time to 10 minutes or so, then back to our rooms, havens in a lot of ways.

Over the following few days gangrene really stuffed any idea that we were in a haven and destroyed any hope of keeping the feet. Ten days before Christmas and it wasn't *if* we would lose the feet but when and how much would get chopped off.

It was about then that they started to get people like Bill Went and Mark Hills in to see us, the prosthetists from the Artificial Limb Centre. This was a time of real shock as we had naturally assumed we would lose the feet just above the demarcation zone down near the ankles where the good tissue started. No such luck. The join between the good tissue and the rotten was pretty dramatic, the nurses tried to keep it covered with gauze dressings but when they were removed you could see the bones and sinews exposed, from where the body has said 'you're not me anymore'.

The first limb that Bill brought in looked like a pasty mummified residual limb, like one modelled out of clay by a kid. Worse it had a tiny stump socket and we had long legs, right down to the ankles in fact. The realisation that we were to be cut off 14 cm below the knee caused great frustration.

'No use going any lower,' we were told, 'you'd only have to have them cut off again, higher up as you get older.'

The real reason was a combination of two things. One, it was thought our vascularisation was compromised low down on the legs due to the cold damage, so the slow healing that is usually associated with lower leg injuries would be even slower. The other consideration was that the fitting of PTB (Patella Tendon Bearing) sockets is far easier on a shorter, conical-shaped stump. Long stumps cause a whole range of problems to the limb fitters but they do have the advantage for the amputee of greater leverage.

This is one of my greatest regrets. Over the last 20 years I have met so many double amputees, predominantly American, with long stumps. Most had almost identical injuries to Phil and myself, and in every case the advantages of living an active life with long stumps have been huge. That leverage is so critical when it comes to skiing, climbing, cycling, all those things that I am passionate about and get so frustrated at not doing well enough.

I'm not sure if we would ever have been able to change the minds of the medical team. They sure as hell thought they had considered every option, but perhaps one of them needed to be a fit young double amputee who wanted to take on the world. By the same token perhaps they didn't and still haven't given me all the information used in making their decision to cut me off that short.

Those were a long 10 days leading up to Christmas. The gangrene was infecting one leg and just when the drugs finally got on top of the infection, the other leg flared up. At the time I was going through periods of high fever and delirium until the antibiotics killed off a few of the bugs. Any quality of life was rapidly disappearing and the ultra-strong drugs were starting to harm the rest of my body — part of the old kill or cure regime I guess.

As part of the learning and acceptance process, the medical team (I use that term because I was never sure who exactly was calling the shots) arranged for some amputees to visit to give us an idea of life *sans* feet. Now from what I understand, they always try to send in someone slightly worse off than you, so we were visited by an older guy, from Ashburton I think. In the tradition of trying to send in someone worse off than you, he was a BK/AK. That is, he had one leg off below the knee (BK) and one leg off above the knee (AK). I can remember him being excited about still being able to climb a ladder onto the roof of his house (and falling off a few times I think).

It reminded me of Middle Peak Hotel when they put Anne on the radio, seemed like a good idea perhaps, but the reality was that it did the opposite of what was intended. What we needed was someone truly inspirational and we were getting closer to that in the books by Sir Douglas Bader and Norman Croucher.

But it was a good try, even if only appreciated for the reality check.

But the question was always: how soon until we are up and out of here, how soon until we can be mobile enough to get back to work?

The advice I have cherished the most came from one of the registrars. He stood at the end of the bed and said, 'This isn't going to magically heal up in weeks or months, this is something that you will learn to master over the coming years, always getting better, even if only incrementally. This is something that is going to be painful and frustrating over the next few months but it will improve week by week.'

I knew even then that it was great advice, some of the first really truthful and complete advice we had. So many others were so busy painting rosy pictures that they possibly discounted the fact that we were intelligent and strong people who actually thrive on a challenge.

Over those weeks the feet went through the stages of degradation and also through what limited healing there was. The changes happening down there at the end of the bed were continuous so I really came to look at the condition of my feet as interesting more than anything. I've always said it's like having your own Discovery Channel or full-colour *National Geographic* article on frostbite. Not everyone felt like that though. To make matters even more uncomfortable for some, I tended to keep the feet hanging out in the breeze as they say. Not for any medical reasons, more just the subtle claustrophobia I live with. I hate being constrained, even now I only buy sleeping bags that have full zips, rarely wear long trousers and love having a window open.

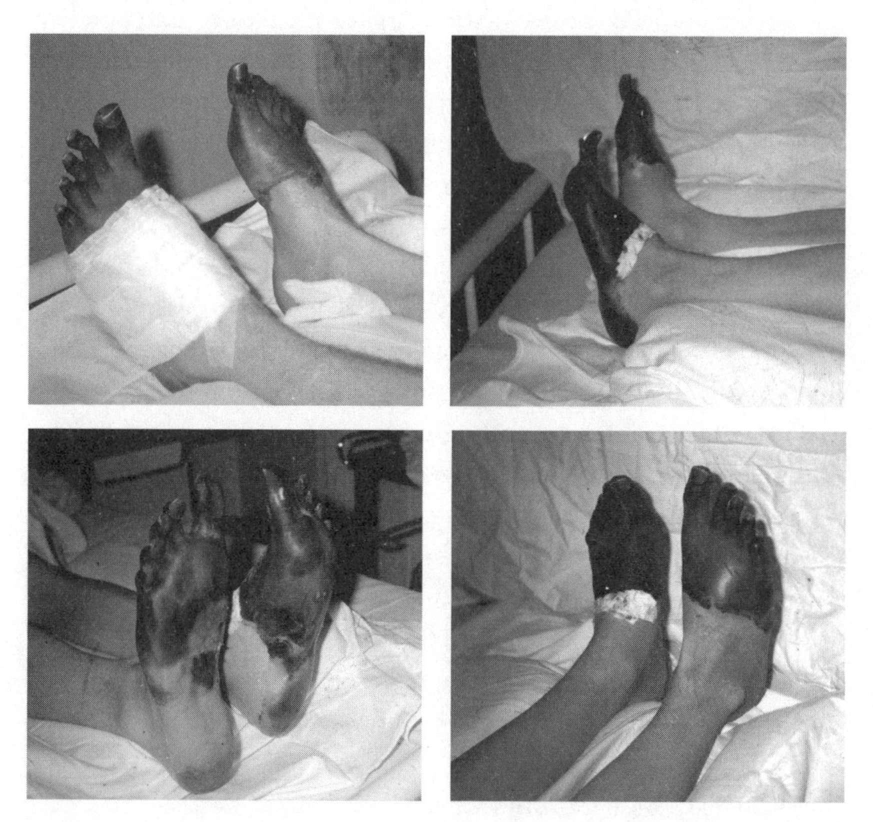

Top left: After two weeks, gangrene and the realisation that more than toes will be lost.
Top right and bottom: Near Christmas Eve, 1982, two feet of little use to anyone – time to go.

With the changes of the feet from their initial white, slightly swollen waxiness, to blue and purple, grossly distended with gangrene, and finally to black and almost mummified, there was always something less than pleasant on show. Visiting hours were a bit of a reality check at times when the visitor, on entering the room and seeing the feet, would turn somewhat white and have to sit down. For a lot of people, seeing the extent of the damage and the condition of the feet in the final stages of frostbite was almost too much. For some people I would make sure my feet were covered, for others I would make sure they were uncovered (ensured a quick visit every time).

They also stopped being part of my body, part of me, especially in the week before Christmas. It was time for them to go and although getting the date of the operation was a shock it was also a relief. I was thinking, 'OK, let's get them off and then we can get on with life.'

Those whole four weeks in hospital were leading to the amputation. We didn't know or accept it at first, but the medical team surely did from day one. Certainly the team back at Mount Cook could all see the extent of the injury and the likely outcome far more clearly than I could. Those weeks were all about doing as much as possible to save the residual limb, to ensure the maximum amount of limb was saved, while, just as importantly, allowing us to understand and accept what was inevitable.

I think for a while I even thought I had some say in the whole deal, until that second round of gangrene set in. The antibiotic drugs I was on were, as one nurse explained, 'top shelf' stuff, very powerful, and the doctors had to tread a fine line between killing off the bugs, the entericoli bacteria causing the gangrene, and killing off my own cells. Every day on those drugs chipped away at some part of my relatively healthy metabolism. They had the potential to cause both liver and kidney damage, so when the second bout of rot set in, there was no choice.

The date was set for 24th December, Christmas Eve.

In one respect the operation was quite straightforward, just a routine amputation really, but complicated by the fact that there were two per person. To have one leg done one week and the other the following week would have been torture, and for one surgeon to do all four legs at once would have been too much for the surgeon and for us (too many hours under general anaesthetic). The result was two teams, a team headed by Stewart Sinclair, our consultant plastic surgeon, working on the left legs and a team headed by Professor Gillespie, the head of orthopaedics in Christchurch, dealing with the right legs.

You know it's real when the 'nil by mouth' sign goes up on the bed head the day before the operation. It was like waiting for a sentence to be handed down, in this case a sentence to be a double amputee for the rest of my life.

Anne was with me for much of the time while I was being weighed and checked over by the anaesthetist. This is the poor sod who has to explain everything, like the chances of your not waking up and, if you do wake up, how crook you will really feel. I had been under a general anaesthetic when I was 15 after a mishap on my motorbike (for those who know motorbikes, I landed badly from a jump, doing a 'flying W' and mashed up my testicles somewhat — still worked though). So I remembered just how ill you feel from the anaesthetic itself, let alone having your legs chopped off.

It was also time for what I still think of as the 'smiley face' to be drawn on the legs. This was the line they were going to cut along, and to see it so far up the leg really rammed home how much they were going to take off.

On a brighter note was the possibility of saving some of my left leg. The frostbite didn't seem to be so invasive in the heel of that foot, giving rise to the chance of a Symes amputation. This is when only the forefoot gets chopped off, leaving the full length of your tibia and fibula connected by your heel. The weight-bearing and leverage advantages of a Symes would have been huge; having the heel pad to support my weight would open up a much greater range of mobility. However, the deal was that I wouldn't know and they wouldn't know until I was on the slab and they could open the foot up for a look. If it looked sound I would get to keep it, but if it looked suspect then the whole leg would go.

Waking up on Christmas Eve morning, feeling hungry and nervous, but I was still able to crack the odd joke. Phil was first, wheeled past my door: 'Good luck, mate, see you tomorrow.'

Then it's 11 am and my turn. The pre-med drugs had started to take effect, leaving me pretty cruisey. I guess they are aimed at relaxing you, getting your metabolism ready to have its lights temporarily turned off. Before theatre all jewellery or anything metal needs to be removed, but as I'd never worn much jewellery I didn't have any to take off (though I would have had a wedding ring to take off if I hadn't accidentally thrown it out with the spud peelings a few months earlier, as Anne reminds me regularly). I had thought that you needed to get rid of the metal so you wouldn't get burnt from arcing if they had to use the 'paddles' to revive you, but it was also because they were to use electronic cauterising of the small veins and nerves during the amputation. So much for being a 'know it all' at the time.

As the pre-med was kicking in I reminded them not to get confused about which leg to keep and could they please measure me so they could get the height right afterwards.

The trip on the trolley was pretty dream-like; I was a bit spaced out, feeling like 'well here goes'; Anne at my side to say, 'See you soon'.

When you are on your back the operating theatre is dominated by the huge lights and people's faces, hidden behind their masks. On the wall I could see what looked like Black and Decker hand tools and cold chisels. All I could think of was: 'Where is the saw and I hope it's sharp.'

10, 9, 8, nothing, oblivion, another three hours of life missing.

Above: Sunset on Aoraki/Mount Cook; East Ridge is on far right.

Below: The Park staff, 1984; I am at bottom left.

Top: SAR team practising, 1981.

Left: The Red Wall, Mount Hicks, 1981; the snow is over 500m below.

Above: Our wedding day 29th August, 1982.

Above: High (left) and Middle Peaks of Mount Cook; East Ridge rises from the right, Middle Peak Hotel is at the start of the ice cliff in the shade, just to the left of East Ridge.

Below: Don Bogie with me in the Bauman stretcher, landing on the Empress Shelf, before returning to get Phil.

Gareth Eyres/*North & South*

Life at Montana Wines.

Left: 'Flying' down the ladders.

Below: Standing on top of a 137,000 litre ferment tank.

Gareth Eyres/*North & South*

4 NEW YEAR, NEW LEGS

CHRISTMAS DAY, 1982, NOT New Year by the calendar, but 'New Year' and a new life for me.

I had woken in the recovery room next to the operating theatre to see some kind faces, had a sip of water, then drifted back into the cloudy murk of unconsciousness. I needed to know if both legs were trans-tibial amputations or if they had managed to save the left leg with a Symes amputation. The theatre nurse told me that both had gone, the surgeon would be around later. The truth of her answer was obvious when I woke later that evening, feeling like shit as you do after those drugs, and feeling pinned to the bed, everything dead from my hips down. As the nurse was propping me up slightly to have a sip of water, the reality of no legs was scarily apparent, the bed sheets went flat half way down the bed. Even with the cradles holding the sheets up, the mound in the bed was still too short.

'Christ, what am I going to do now?'

I really thought I had come to accept my fate, my new being, before the operation but I realised then that it was only just starting. If only it could have been an accident, if only I hadn't needed to go through those weeks of initial hope, then the grieving and what I thought was acceptance of the inevitable. All I could think, could say to myself was, 'Crap, all for bloody nothing, I really don't have legs.'

Worse still was the feeling of being pinned to the bed. I am sure claustrophobia contributed to the feeling of despair that was sweeping over me in waves, just as the nausea was sweeping through my body, objecting to the general anaesthetic. Christ, I felt like crap, no use telling me it would get better soon, it was terrible right there and then and damn hard to see my way out of it.

What a night. Not that I saw much of it anyway, just enough to feel sorry for myself then back into a drug-induced sleep until 25th December 1982. What a terrible day. I could finally see the plaster casts that now encased my legs from my upper thighs down, mind you, not all that far down — they sure looked short.

Before the operation, in an effort to try to understand, to accept what was going to happen, I tried to learn as much as possible about the amputation, how they were going to do it, what bones would be left and what shapes, what muscles would be left, where the suture/stitch line would be and what would happen after they were cut off.

Well, not much of it registered, although I'm sure all the information was ticking away in my subconscious, so it probably would have been worse without that info.

What did I wake up to?

They had taken both legs off 14 cm below the knee. They had made a cut like a big smile across the front of the shin and peeled back the skin at the front and the calf muscle and skin at the rear. In doing the cuts they had to cauterise heaps of capillaries and veins, stitch up or seal arteries, and sever and seal nerves that used to service my toes, feet, ankles and lower legs. The bones needed to be cut off with the tibia (the one at the front, your shin bone) longer than the fibula at the back. The bones needed to be chipped and ground down to taper the edges before sewing the whole deal up to shape the stump. I'm sure that to be a successful orthopaedic surgeon you need to be a cross between a 'chippy' or carpenter and an iron man — it looks hard work. This whole procedure was the antithesis of Stewart Sinclair's work as a reconstructive surgeon. I think you could see it in him in the last days before the legs came off; he was used to building, to repairing, not to demolition.

The stump gets formed by wrapping the residual calf muscle around the base of the cut tibia and then sewing it up. As they close the stump up two drain lines are placed in the wound, one in deep, right through the centre, near the base of the cut and the other just under the suture line. These are connected to a vacuum tube and excess fluid is drained away, speeding up healing.

Normally the stumps are wrapped in dressings and pressure bandages to control swelling and infection, with the dressings being changed regularly (twice per day), and the wrapping of the pressure bandages helping to determine the final shape of the stump; a real art and bloody painful from all accounts.

For us though something new, plaster casts for weeks on end, no peeking under the bandages but also no stump bandaging. The swelling that occurs after any major trauma such as this was to be controlled by the drains and the rigid plaster casts. As long as everything was sterile when wrapped up in theatre, the wounds would remain that way and the stumps would be the shape determined by Bill Went and Mark Hills (the limb fitters) in the theatre, not by someone doing the daily wrapping. I'll never know whether it was an advantage, I do know that it took some time to get to grips with the heavy casts.

The next three days, the 25th, 26th and 27th of December, were the blackest days of my life, not even Anne, Mum or Dad could console me. It wasn't so much the fact that I'd lost my legs but the whole rising up out of the drug murk. The pain was there from the start, but so were the pethidine and other drugs. I was paranoid about getting hooked on morphine-type drugs while at the same time desperately needing them. But they are a double-edged sword all right. They take away the pain, and terrible pain it was at times (just like you'd had your legs chopped off, in fact), but at the same time they also take away your interest in life, leaving you mentally and physically lethargic.

Not only do you not want to move your body but your bowels decide they are anaesthetised as well and stop moving, bunging you right up. It's bad enough needing help to go to the toilet in a pan in your bed, but when you *can't* go it's even worse. Having to eat stuff that tastes like bird food then having it roar straight out the other end an hour later, messing the bed, or getting so bunged up that the only thing that will unblock you is one of those health professionals who earn every cent they get paid. It was so humiliating, so degrading, I spent more time in those days apologising than conversing. As well as all that, moving hurt, so you really didn't want to, but being pinned down and not moving just made everything even worse.

Stewart Sinclair came in to see Phil and me on Christmas Day which I really appreciated. He sat for a while and described the operation and how positive he was about the outcome. The downside of his visit was that he brought one of his children. I hadn't let Anne bring Lucy in as I really felt I couldn't deal with a wee kid in any shape or form, even my own loved one. So once the little Sinclair started pulling on the drain lines attached to the most sensitive part of my body at the time, I started to freak out. 'Whoa, call the kid off please.'

I had just lost my legs but I was almost more concerned about ruining everyone's Christmas Day and not being able to stomach Christmas lunch and pudding. The only consolation was that it was rather ghastly rolled turkey and canned peas, but I still drooled over it shortly before throwing up.

It wasn't until the third day or so that life started to flood back into me. Getting used to the routine of this new phase of my life, of being monitored for what went into my mouth and what came out of my body via drains and other orifices, accepting the inevitability of being pinned down, and the first stirrings of ambition all combined with decreasing levels of severe pain to lift the dark clouds somewhat.

I know now that that first week was setting new standards in my life for feeling like crap. It was testing me and I wasn't handling it with the courage and grace I thought I would. Not that I got an 'E' for effort or anything but I'm sure I could do better now I've had some practice at it.

As the days went by, it was like lifting out of the clouds. I was focused on that drain, monitoring the amount of fluid coming out as carefully as the nurses. Every day it decreased, which was a great sign, as I would soon be off it and mobile. Mobility came first in bath and toilet chairs, I had to be pushed around in them but at least I was up. After weeks of lying down I would get dizzy easily when sitting up or moving around. The bed became home, a haven, a sanctuary. While I had thought I really had my act together in the weeks before the amputation, it was Phil who bounced back the quickest after the operation. I was always lagging a day or so, more perhaps, in the milestones of our recovery. Perhaps it was those terrible first few days of being humiliated with constipation, perhaps it was just me.

Slowly mobility came back, the drugs dropped to a few morphine- and codeine-based tablets each day and during the night. It wasn't easy to reduce them, they are such a powerful form of satiety that while they take away pain, they also take away motivation and 'spark', lessening your drive to recover. A difficult cycle to break.

Physiotherapy started early with upper body strengthening, something Phil embraced more than me. He had retained more muscle from our time on the hill, giving him a lead on the simplest of exercises, quite depressing at times, quite motivating (in a beat the bastard sort of way) at other times.

After 14 days it was time to change the plaster casts. I didn't quite know what to expect as I was unconscious (thank goodness) when the casts went on. I hadn't asked Anne to come along, or, at least, she didn't know about it. The casts were to be removed, the drains pulled out of the wounds, the dressings changed and new casts fitted, this time with sockets in them for basic pylon legs.

No general anaesthetic for this, just some gas, some nitrous oxide, the stuff dentists use. One of the nurses (also an Anne) came with me from the ward, hanging onto my hand and chatting as a good friend does, though I repaid her by almost breaking her fingers. I was feeling nervous as they cut the casts off using one of those vibrating saws that only cut the plaster, not the patient. I was sucking on some gas to stay calm and to relieve some of the pain from the vibration and pressure on the still-healing stump. No problem I thought, remove the casts and then the dressings and then start on the sutures holding in the drains. The first drain was painful but OK, big sucks on the gas sure helped out, but the second drain felt as though they were pulling my testicles out with a claw hammer. The pain was excruciating, never in my life has anything hurt so much. It wasn't just one pull but several, until someone realised they had left a suture in attaching the end of the drain to the wound. So in fact, as I pointed out, they were attempting to pull my stump inside out. Nurse Anne's hand got squeezed so hard I was sure I had done some damage. Mercifully they turned the gas flow up, and I sucked so hard I temporarily passed out. Not for long enough though, as we still had another stump to do.

Certainly the Gold standard for pain so far in my life, and one standard I never want exceeded.

The other stump was almost worse, it didn't hurt as much as the first one, but the anticipation of that pain coming back was actually pretty freaky — no one wants that sort of stuff to happen again, unless they're really twisted of course.

Everyone seemed pretty pleased with how the stumps looked, no signs of infection, as there shouldn't have been with the gobs of antibiotics we had consumed. After cleaning and redressing with large foam cups covering the ends of the stumps, new casts were applied, once again right up my thighs. The main difference, apart from having no drains to tie us to the beds, were leg attachments set into the plaster.

These were the 'pylon' attachments, just like on 'real' prosthetic legs, set up so that short tube legs could be fitted enabling us to do limited upright walking between parallel bars in the rehabilitation gym. I think this was to show us some progress in order to lift our spirits, and also to get our bodies upright and starting to work after seven weeks of lying down.

It was also now time to move out into the wards; more deserving patients needed the isolated rooms we had, burns victims and other patients in for plastic surgery.

By this time Burwood had become home, my family. Day excursions out would inevitably end up with my asking Anne, 'When are we going home?' I'd read and heard about the dependence that long-stay patients develop (children especially), when the hospital community replaces their families. In many ways that community, that hospital family, does become more important than your own, as they are the ones who share your every minute, all your pain and pain relief, your highs and lows, frequently some of the most dramatic times of your life. I could see it happening. It was a bit like the drug-dependence concerns for me; while you are aware and attempting to manage and avoid the situation, it starts to take over anyway.

It was about this time that a bit of medical paranoia on my part crept in. In the days following the re-casting of my stumps and legs I was beginning to feel as though something wasn't right. A continual nagging pain, a hot itchiness bugged me constantly, so like all determined patients I bugged the staff. It went further than that though. I became obsessed with the idea my stump was rotting, I was sure I could smell it, I could definitely feel it. Although the thermometers said otherwise, I was sure I had a fever, I couldn't sleep for worry. What 'it' was I wasn't certain but I wanted it fixed. Eventually they agreed to cut the cast off and have a look, while indicating that it was pretty much a waste of time. I think I said something like if that's all that's wasted then no problem.

Sure enough, a healthy stump well on the way to healing was unveiled, then promptly wrapped up again. I was too relieved to feel like a right chump, though it probably took me days to stop saying sorry.

For me the great benefit in being at Burwood was that as soon as I started to feel more human and mobile, the option to move into the attached spinal unit came up. Both Phil and I were away as soon as we had our own wheelchairs. We were moved into the dormitory-style wards with the spinal patients. They were predominantly young males like us, recovering from falls, motorbike and rugby accidents, and all those other things that break your back. It was there that I learnt heaps about spirit, about how lucky I was to only be a temporary guest there. What a change from the wards, where patients deal with trauma, recover and leave in a relatively short space of time. The guys in the spinal unit were there to learn a new way of life, a new way of 'being'. No magic cures; for some a gradual and continual increase in function, for others almost the opposite. The trials these guys went through, were going through, made what we were facing look like a Christmas outing.

I still wasn't doing enough in the gym. I really couldn't see much sense in messing around with the pylons on the casts, as we could really take very little weight on the stumps and without knee movement the 'walking' was pretty ugly. As usual Phil persevered to a greater extent than me, but it was very much a 'hurry up and move on, please' stage.

That next stage was the removal of the large leg casts once again, and for the last time, thank god. Short stump socket casts were made to wear around in the wheelchair to control swelling until our first 'legs' were made. The first of many fittings involved, as it still does, a detailed plaster cast being taken of the stump, then a model of the stump being formed from it. From that model, the prosthetists create, through art and science, the socket into which all your weight will be transferred when you are upright and walking. To this they temporarily fix a 'jig' with a foot attached for the initial fitting, to get all the angles right. Once that is done it's back to the workshop where the jig is removed and the final leg built up to the measurements taken. Sounds easy, but as we were to learn, there is no such thing as perfection in this craft.

Having had those two very different surgeons operate on separate legs meant two different styles of stump, and two very different shapes were formed. I loved the idea of the meaty stump left by Stewart Sinclair but quickly learnt that it was going to prove more difficult to make a socket with. The ideal for the limb fitter is a conical shape, pretty much what I had on the right side, not the bulbous thing on the left. But no matter how hard it would be to fit, I was sure that having muscle there must be a good thing in the long term.

The other great bonus of the spinal unit was that as soon as I had lost the full casts Anne and I got to move into one of their motel-style units until it was time to leave. It was our first time together for about 10 weeks, so we had plenty to catch up on. We quickly learnt that life as a double amputee had some complications, some learning would have to go on, as a back injury after the first few nights indicated. I won't tell you whose or how — I'll leave that to the many active imaginations out there.

There was a gradual weaning away from hospital life. The New Year had been and gone, it was time for me to be gone as well.

While such dramatic events fill your life, your days dealing with them become normal, the standard. But the rest of life needs to go on, cannot be ignored. We still needed money to live. I was in hospital in my own little world, but every day Anne dipped into that world and then went back to coping with the outside world. Our New Zealand accident compensation system was a life-line for us, providing four days' wages a week. In many ways we were lucky that we had been so engrossed in our lifestyle at Mount Cook, where you can't own a house, that we had little debt and low rent on our isolated and subsidised housing. As I hadn't had much in the way of sick days in my years at the park they kindly made up the extra day per week, effectively removing another source of stress from our unusual lifestyle. By the time Phil and I were ready to leave hospital, ACC had been convinced by our doctors and friends that our lump sum payment ($17,000 in 1983) could be paid out without us having to wait years. It was determined that the extent of our injuries was fairly clear cut, obvious in fact. That meant funds were available for Anne and me to get a reliable car and some independence.

But where to go from hospital?

Where else, back to Mount Cook, back to our home and hopefully back to a useful job. Both Phil and I had been promised jobs back with the Lands and Survey Department, very generous offers we both took up: Phil back to surveying, myself back to being the duty ranger at Cook.

Before leaving hospital we were advised to get hand controls for our cars, once again evidence of people underestimating the ability of the human body and mind to adapt. Being somewhat bloody minded we practised driving an automatic car in the hospital car park with the help of a walking stick. Not recommended in traffic, of course, but fun. I drove out of that place in February 1983, driving our old manual Holden and except for a few years with an automatic I've driven a manual ever since.

When first back at Cook, I tried to make like a house-husband, looking after Lucy while Anne worked. Some of the time was spent in the wheelchair, the rest up on the legs.

I started work again with a few hours per day and increased gradually. Mostly at that time I worked at the front counter, giving climbing advice and helping tourists with questions, still itching to get out of the office.

The first challenge as a double amputee was managing the rapidly changing stumps, each shrinking by the day, which meant the fit of those early legs changed dramatically every week. Living back at Mount Cook village meant that I rapidly became an expert at leg socket alterations.

Being a new double amputee was, looking back, all consuming. I also had some problems with people's attitudes to me. When you think about it, it was really only a change in body and lifestyle from the knees down, but the approach most people (other than those close to me) took was that it had changed me as a person, as if my personality and 'being' had been cut out, rather than just my legs amputated. That approach, that attitude to me, rubs off and I find that even if it's only a little it actually slows you down in getting on with life at 110 per cent.

The images of those years for me are very much of getting the strands of life back together, of being able to earn a living, explore the limits of the new lifestyle and expunge some of the ghosts of November 1982.

Every morning for the first six months it was necessary to follow an almost unvarying ritual. Once up, I would remove the night casts. These were plaster casts that fitted firmly over the stumps and were held on by a 'suspender belt'. The object of going to bed every night with a suspender belt on was to stop overnight swelling of the stumps, giving me a head start in getting the legs on in the morning. Once up, normally in the wheelchair or an armchair, it was time to start putting on the legs. Some days it was with real trepidation and frustration, other days it couldn't happen soon enough, depending on the level of pain and frustration of the day before. The sockets were just hard fibreglass, the stump socks thick woollen socks. As my stumps were quite new, every night they would swell up so I would start the day with one or two socks and be up to three or four layers within a few hours as the stumps shrunk. After a month or two, the sock count would be up as high as eight. Now multiply this by two for both stumps and you have a hell of a lot of socks to wash in the ringer washing machine each day. I got so sick of putting socks through the ringer, trying to dry them on a winter's day at Mount Cook (or a summer's day for that matter).

Once up and going it was milestone after milestone: going from two walking sticks to one; walking all the way up the village to the shop; then managing the walk home; the first whole day back at work — the milestones just ticked on by.

I was still carrying a lot of guilt for getting myself, Phil and, even more importantly, my family into the situation I found myself in. Still uncharted territory for everyone, not just me, it was really quite pioneering stuff both physically and emotionally. Anne and Lucy, as well as my close friends Bob and Anne Munro, gave me no leeway for self-pity. There were days when I craved a good dose of pity, would have been happy sulking away and being waited on hand and foot (well not foot perhaps). But no way, it was very much a case of pull your weight, mate.

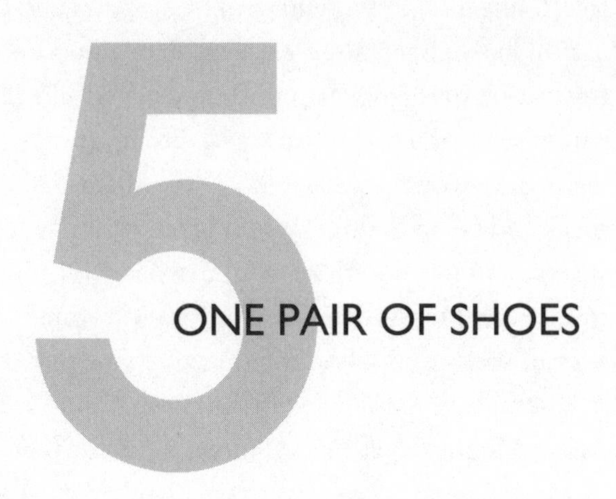

5 ONE PAIR OF SHOES

ANNE AND I, WITH Lucy and later Jeremy (born January 1985), settled back into life at Mount Cook village for another 18 months. The time went fast, as we were all learning again, in a familiar and challenging environment. Early on I bought a three-wheeled Honda ATV, the trike for getting around the park and village.

One of my duties had always been to help out with rabbit control in the park, conducting night shoots, mainly with Gnome at the wheel of the 'Rhino Catcher', his park plumber's truck. A freezing night spent being bounced around the glacial flats, trying to reduce the population of hares and rabbits, was always the highlight of the week. Needless to say, rabbit featured in many different forms on the table at dinnertime.

The trike was seen in places conservationists would cringe at now, but it got me out and about without trashing my stumps or enthusiasm. It was quite a commitment and somewhat in the pioneering spirit to be way up the Ball Hut road knowing that if I fell off or broke down it was going to be hell to get back home.

Most visitors to the park hadn't seen a double amputee before, especially not one wearing shorts, which I did a lot. In fact the more able I became, the more comfortable I was wearing shorts in public, as I automatically wore them at home. It was, and still is, just so much easier to tighten the legs, slip them off and on to add another sock, and just generally to move around in shorts. While living at Mount Cook, it wasn't much of an issue anyway. We rarely spent any time in crowded towns and shops, and the locals were all used to the weird and wonderful anyway, as that's the type of people attracted to hideaways like the village, so a legless ranger was of no consequence to them.

Same for my children. As each of them has grown up, they have gone through phases of adapting to Dad's unusual situation. From the earliest stages of my recovery the artificial legs have been a focus for children. Leave a set of legs lying around and I guarantee that within a few minutes the nearest child will be playing with them, usually trying them on. It's common to see children hopping around our house with their knee in the socket of a leg, making like an amputee. By the same token, my children are constantly bemused by the attention I sometimes attract: 'Hell, it's only Dad' is the sentiment, I think.

A popular sport in the family developed from our first trips out of Mount Cook, especially to city streets and malls. While I walked, the family would follow 10 metres behind me, continually amused by the reactions of the public. Naturally enough kids are always the most open, adults the most embarrassed. Half-finished sentences follow me around malls, airports and such, like: 'Mummy, look at that . . .' then 'Shhhhhh' and the poor little sods get choked by their parents as they drag them away in a state of embarrassment.

At home I always take the legs off to help heal the inevitable damage to one stump or the other. To get around without my legs on I generally walk on my knees, unless I'm outside on concrete or coarsely textured surfaces when I hop around on my bum. Needless to say if there are kids around they will imitate me, motoring around on their knees to try it out.

Stairs in our various houses have always attracted attention too, as without my legs the fastest way to get down by far is to slide on my bum. I quickly became a connoisseur of stairs (as did the kids); they aren't all created equal by any means. For a start the tread dimensions and the steepness of the stairs determine the speed. Next most important factor is the tread covering. Wooden stairs are brutal and I won't even mention splinters. Carpet is the optimum covering for speed and control. While the kids slide down in sleeping bags, I'm generally in my underwear (or less — not a pleasant thought I know), so I need to be aware of the material interactions. Good quality woollen carpet (as long as it doesn't have protruding tacks) is a pleasure to zoom down. The straightness of your body controls speed. High speed descents are achieved when you lie almost flat, skimming over the treads; the slowest descents are when you sit up and bump down each step. Nylon underwear can heat up somewhat on a long flight, and the combination of nylon carpet and underwear is almost lethal. In fact, as I have found out, nylon carpet can inflict a nasty burn at even the slowest speeds. When sliding is out, then some climbing techniques come in handy: 'bridging' with both arms on opposing walls enables you to almost hop down, taking several treads at once. All essential skills I have passed on to the kids.

As mobility and confidence increased, I got about on a mountain bike more and more. I installed a child seat on the back and, until Lucy got too big (and that took a while), we were the terrors of the walking tracks in the Hooker Valley. The occasional prang didn't seem to phase the two-year-old too much, not that she had a lot of choice, being strapped in and wearing a helmet that spent half the time down over her eyes.

I still wasn't fully active in my role as duty ranger; the talks I loved to do, but I didn't always feel competent leading the longer interpretive walks. The biggest perk as duty ranger was getting to hoon (sorry, drive) around in the Landcruiser. The hand over from your seven-day shift as duty ranger was always in the Tavern Bar after the last 7 pm radio 'sched' of your shift. The 'retiring' duty ranger could then make up for the week's moderation in alcohol while the new inductee had to control himself for a whole week, not always easy at Mount Cook in those days.

I guess every small community goes through phases where everyone just clicks, making the community especially strong and fun to be part of. That's what the village was like for most of the time Anne and I lived there, though it was hard for Anne at times, not being a climber and having small children to look after (though not all on her own), as there just weren't that many families to interact with.

The focal point of the village was the Tavern Bar every Friday (at least) night. The whole village, kids and all, used to pack in that tiny bar from 5 or so until late. Drinking, darts, socialising, dreaming and scheming all went on there. Climbing plans were hatched, and sometimes, conveniently or otherwise, forgotten the next morning. Frequently too much beer or wine was consumed, always regretted the next day.

Darts would often develop into a game of chicken, the throwing of darts between an opponent's feet. Well you can imagine the looks of visitors when my 'friends' would fire the darts directly into the top of my feet — very amusing at times. For me, drinking too much always led to the true expression of the term 'legless' as the first thing to go was always my balance, rapidly followed by anything resembling good sense.

Things were far from rosy a lot of the time though. Pain was a frequent visitor most days, especially during those first two years. The old saying 'no pain, no gain' was never more correct. The only way to get ahead was to push the boundaries, just as in training any part of your body. In cycling and all sports the training effect on your physiology is all about compensation for overuse. The strain-and-recover theme of training is really about getting your body to adapt to new situations; it's just the overuse part that damages both the body and mind at times. For many athletes like myself, getting us to rest is more difficult than going hard. When athletes complain about how they 'hurt' from doing a run or a cycle, they should try it as an amputee, then they would really know hurt.

To block out that hurt I frequently used alcohol. A few beers would work a damn sight better that some of the pain medication, and yes, quite often it would be a few too many, maybe to work on the psychological pain that I still hadn't finished working through.

While there were great times, there were also times of intense sadness, as is the way in the mountains. Deaths of friends came too regularly, but that's climbing I guess. When people face significant challenges, participate in true sports, then the 'quid pro quo' is danger.

Neal Whiston ('Whist') died in an unfortunate and simple accident; the brilliant climber tripped and hit his head while on an easy climb showing friends the mountains he loved. Digger, who delivered those first bags to us on Middle Peak with Ron, died in a ski-plane crash on the Tasman Glacier. Digger had been like a father to me, a mentor, an intensely caring person who had a bottomless well of concern for others and love for life.

It was terribly frustrating not to be able to be actively involved in their accidents, their rescues. Some may think it a blessing not to be actively involved, but I always saw involvement as a tool for coping with the trauma. It was at that stage I realised I was more a voyeur than a participant, something that always leaves me unsettled. It was time to go, to make the break from the safety and security of Mount Cook and move out into what we always considered the 'outside world'.

But what to do? I applied for a job managing a new climbing shop and guiding operation for friends but lost out to a more experienced person, luckily as it turned out as the retail part of the operation didn't last that long. I had a great affinity for native flora, so Anne and I tried to buy a plant nursery and garden centre. But without a specialist education or enough cash, the answer after doing the numbers was always no. We either needed heaps of cash, which wasn't going to happen, or I needed an education. After negotiating with ACC we struck a deal where I would enrol in a 'professional' degree, one leading towards a definite career or job prospect and they would support the family at about the same level as the dole.

I picked the Bachelor of Horticulture degree that was being offered by my old university, Lincoln. The worry was that I was only eligible for retrospective enrolment — without the required prerequisites I had to pass all the first year's subjects otherwise my name would be wiped off, as if I had never been there, a complete waste of a year if that happened. I was very weak in the science subjects; I had successfully avoided them at school to do easier subjects and go climbing, so it was time to learn something. Two months before going I bought the dreaded chemistry and biochemistry texts for the next year and every evening I would spend two or three hours studying in the spare room, starting at page one.

Well the two months got me to chapter three I think, not even into the body of the texts. March 1985 came and it was time for school. We moved from our new three-bedroom home at Mount Cook into a disused supermarket, converted into a barely habitable student flat in the centre of Lincoln township. The section full of old trees and a great vegetable garden softened the change from a warm, almost-new house to the pretty basic old shop.

Money was always going to be a problem, as it always has been for students; no different for us. ACC provided the basic means of support and I worked at the local Country Club on the door and behind the bar for a few nights a week to supplement the income. With two children under five, Anne had limited opportunities for work.

School was the biggest surprise, with those months of study at Mount Cook paying huge dividends. The whole basis of the science was understanding basic principles really well and then applying them. I was constantly amazed that a lot of the students straight from seventh form at school didn't have the basics, many had a very poor grasp of even basic mathematics.

I started the year knowing the commitment I had made for both my family and myself, so I tried to put in at least eight hours a day, treating it just like a job. While my grades were good, which was a pleasant validation of all the hours, exam time was never pretty, with some serious nerves showing at times.

From the start I enjoyed the learning as much as any particular subject, it was fascinating and exciting. If my school teachers had known how taken I was by science, especially biochemistry, I bet they would have been saying, 'I told you so.' In fact I quickly realised that if I wanted to continue on with biochemistry the following year I would need to change to the Bachelor of Agricultural Science option. Even better, I would then get to do animal physiology, closer than I had ever dreamt to my growing secret ambition to be a doctor. I knew for my family's sake I couldn't really do it — I had left it too late (and I had been told that I wouldn't be able to handle the walking). To get there I would have needed to do a good biological science degree before I could get entry, all too expensive and time consuming for me. I lapped up the biochemistry in year two, with my trademark passion and obsession showing through strongly. After studying my options I changed my course again to a joint University of Canterbury and Lincoln degree, the Bachelor of Science with Honours in Biochemistry. To make my life even harder, to get entry to the programme I had to do the full third year and three second-year papers as well. Of course it was the dreaded retrospective entry again; pass well or you are out with no credit. A difficult year, especially the more abstract chemistry papers I had to travel into Christchurch for. But once again, I did the hours, did the work, and passed. The final year was spent both at Lincoln as the only student in the programme and at the Christchurch School of Medicine doing my Honours research on Heparin Cofactor Two, one of the anti-clotting agents in human blood.

In those last two years Anne and I built a home in Lincoln, scraping up the money for a deposit with help from relations. And I really mean scraping — our deposit was delivered to the builders in the last minutes before our option ran out, paid in cheques, notes and coins, right down to a bag of one- and two-cent pieces.

During those four years at Lincoln we went through a rollercoaster of emotions from celebrating the birth of our third child, Amanda, in 1989, to sitting up on all-night vigils beside Jeremy's bed in hospital after a serious bowel blockage that necessitated surgery. On the bright side for Jeremy, the surgeon who opened him up was a climber I had rescued once at Mount Cook, so he whipped out his appendix while he was in there, as a thank you. (Well it isn't much use anyway.)

We strove to get ahead in those years like any young family, but life for me was never quite good enough (still isn't) and I needed to look for ways and means of improving it. I was hampered by the late start to my education, always seeming to be five or six years behind my friends. Financially we were always on the edge, and sold our wee house in Lincoln to help pay the debt built up over four years of school before I started on my research job at the Christchurch School of Medicine. There were lots of occasions when I would think of climbing again, but the expense of kitting myself out for alpine climbing was, as always, prohibitive.

While at Lincoln we never lost contact with Mount Cook or its people. While trips back to visit friends like Bob and Anne Munro and their children Hayden and Bridie were restricted to once or twice a year, Gnome (Gary) and Miriam Rees lived close by in Prebbleton. Gnome and Miriam (with their kids, Joel, Aaron and Karl whose ages fell around Lucy and Jeremy's) escaped at a similar time to us, Gnome working as a water supervisor at one of the local Christchurch councils, then later going into business for himself with his trade, plumbing. They had shared our best and worst times at Mount Cook, shared many of the same close friends, lost many of the same close friends. It was Gnome who cared for me in those first hours off the mountain, even if he couldn't find a vein to measure my pulse. Gnome and I always tried to get together on a Friday or in the weekend, with our families sharing meals.

Gnome was with me at Rapaki rock on the Port Hills for one of my first times back rock climbing. We had chosen one of the basic routes, still requiring ropes and harnesses, and the consequences of a fall on that 10-metre high face would have been very serious. As I crested the ridge after grovelling up the face, I took off my harness, one of the few remaining pieces of gear left from Middle Peak Hotel, and gave it to Gnome: 'Here, mate, take this, I don't need it now. I can still do it [rock climb] but it's time to move on to other things.'

Every morning when I put on my legs I was (and still am) reminded of the fact that I live a life of compromise and, at the same time, of how lucky I am. It really is like living with only one pair of shoes to choose from, irrespective of what you want to do that day. The sockets of those legs became the focus of my life: my ability day by day was, and is, determined through those sockets.

Even living close to the Limb Centre in Christchurch I still found it a necessity of life to do all the small repairs and adjustments to my sockets myself. The Limb Centre had moved from its old church-like buildings in the Riccarton Rehabilitation Centre to new purpose-built premises out at Burwood Hospital. On every visit I met people who did no adjustments themselves. How frustrating, I thought, if it was me I would need to be visiting them at least every week. Almost every week I would be adding some packing to the liners of the socket, or else grinding or slicing some off, as my stumps and socks changed. At this time the legs were still the PTB style (Patella Tendon Bearing), still with my beloved old-fashioned leather knee cuffs holding them on, but they now had shock-absorbing liners between my stumps and the fibreglass-style socket. This made fine-tuning the legs much easier. I still needed to grind down the socket in some places where it was rubbing (or make a quick trip to the Limb Centre to get them to do it), but most of the adjustments involved adding packing onto the outside of the liners. Previously I had been adding an increasing number of pairs of socks as my stumps shrunk, but by then most of the dramatic shrinkage had occurred and it was just fine-tuning, perhaps two or three pairs at the most. These socks could be put on the outside of the liner, and cut to reflect the changing shape, allowing for tissue shrinkage and pressure points over bones. New legs were still needed every 18 months or so because the sockets were worn out and also the lower limb/feet components were definitely thrashed about.

New legs were always a double-edged sword, the anticipation huge, the execution frequently disappointing. I nearly always needed new legs because the old ones were not performing, meaning that they were not comfortable and their shape had changed enough to make any further alterations unsuccessful. That is, they were bloody painful and frustrating.

So why the frequent disappointment with new ones? Well, it's a bit like buying one of those old-style leather cycle saddles. Everyone used to swear by how comfortable they were, how good they were, but forgot to mention that before they performed as promised they needed to be 'broken in' by the butt that was going to use them, not any old butt but the exact one attached to the purchaser.

New legs are custom made. The first step in making them is for the limb fitter to carefully measure and mark the stump, then make a very specific plaster cast. From the cast and measurements, a model of your flesh and bone stump is created and, using that model, the new sockets are made. These are attached to temporary lower limb components with fittings that allow enough movement for the limb fitter to adjust the angles of the new limb to attain a natural gait. These new sockets are never perfect, and while you and the limb fitter, as a team, spend hours adjusting the fit, they are still like that new saddle, they need many hours of wearing and fiddling to break them in. After the last fitting you are often buzzing; the fit is great, you've walked hours on them, and you wait with anticipation for the finished article. Traditionally it is then that they get their cosmetics done, an attempt to fool yourself and others that they are real. Then after one or two weeks the new legs arrive. I have never been one of those people who can wear them for an hour or two a day for a few weeks, slowly getting your stumps used to the new sockets and the sockets slowly fashioned to your stump. It's too frustrating and it prolongs the pain anyway, I reckon. I'm definitely a 'throw the old ones away and commit yourself fully to the new ones' man. It causes a few tantrums inevitably, bleeding stumps and the occasional ulcer (stump not stomach) but it gets you up and going faster. There was always some reason to ditch the old ones, so why wait and put up with them any longer.

Once you start to 'break in' the legs and stumps the incremental advances in ability come. Only once do I believe I went backwards in ability with a new set of legs, so they didn't last long.

The legs really get a thrashing at times; every amputee has a collection of stories, generally pulled out when trying to upstage one another at the limb centre on a busy day. For my part, not making it to a limb centre very often meant not quite enough maintenance, which resulted in some interesting situations at times. On the way to one of my first public speaking opportunities, Anne and I decided I really did need new shoes. Now I hadn't actually taken the shoes off that particular set of legs since new, about six months previously. So it was something of a surprise and an embarrassment when I whipped off the shoes in front of the shoe salesman only to find the sock completely rotted off from the ankle down. Haven't worn socks since.

The maintenance problem could be more catastrophic though. While guiding a three-year-old Lucy across the street in Geraldine one afternoon, the left ankle snapped, with the foot completely falling off. With traffic coming from both directions, and me sitting on my arse in the middle of the road, Lucy calmly picked up the foot, gave me her hand and led me off the street.

It is probably quite fortunate that I am a double amputee by frostbite, otherwise I am sure I would have at least one self-administered amputation by the wood-chopping axe. For years, like most Mainland Kiwis, Anne and I have had homes heated by some sort of fire, necessitating annual firewood pilgrimages. I have always had a love affair with axes and chainsaws, and I get all excited at the very idea of firewood cutting, plus it also provides me with an almost therapeutic pastime. It must be in the genes, as I'm sure Dad always has at least five years of firewood stacked up somewhere. Wood chopping as a double amputee is twice the fun, no more worries about aiming that axe, or about being overzealous with that chainsaw — a leg won't grow back but it can be rebuilt.

At least once a month, more often if pushing life hard, I would get a reminder that come the morning there was only one choice. Pressure sores, infected hair follicles or just plain zits, call them what you like, but if they are on a pressure-sensitive part of the stump (which they always are) then it makes for a bad start to the day. You can't, or shouldn't, butcher your sockets for just one zit, but at the same time there is no way my life is going to stop. So the only answer is to work really hard to clear it up, and walk carefully. It is always at the start and the end of the day that it really hurts — in between it's just annoying.

That's life with one pair of shoes.

6 LEGS FOR EVERY OCCASION

NOW YOU CAN APPROACH life as an amputee from several angles. One way is to ignore the fact that you are missing a limb and carry on with life; a very useful way of overcoming many of the prejudices associated with disablement of any type, you just get on with it. Another way is to look at your condition as a new blank sheet and see if you can't work out better ways of doing things. I'm definitely the sort of guy who falls into the latter class.

Now I'm a bit of a gear freak, doesn't matter whether it is cycling, mountaineering or skiing, if it's a passion, then I love embracing the weird, the new, and often the extreme tools and technology. This can at times reinforce those subconscious inhibitions or fences that both you and others can put up as barriers, but equally it can lead to new and very exciting developments.

Skiing was the first sport I encountered that really needed some technology with the legs. While still at living at Mount Cook I was lucky enough to do some cross-country skiing in the winters, down around the village. I was a bit hesitant to go high into the alps for the simple reason that I wasn't sure enough of getting myself all the way out again. Also I had left nearly all the climbing gear that I owned in Middle Peak Hotel, now all lost to the mountain and the glaciers (should pop out of the bottom of the Hooker Glacier some time in the next few years, please return anything that you find). We weren't in a financial position to replace my equipment either. With a young family and a disability to come to grips with, high alpine climbing was certainly a low priority for me. Without the driving need to climb high again, I substituted skiing and cycling for climbing: not as good, not the same level of extreme challenge and satisfaction, but close at times.

The first few times on downhill skis were at Tekapo's Round Hill field, the field I had learnt on as a kid. But it's not quite as easy as just stepping into boots and skis and then pointing them down a hill. Being the gear freak that I am, I gave the idea a lot of thought (too much actually, but never mind that). I decided that weight was going to be a critical issue — quite right as it turned out but about number three after several other issues though. I sourced a second-hand pair of Scott boots, ultra thin light-weight boots made 20 years ago. I had to stuff my very rigid wood and fibreglass legs into these, not easy I can assure you. Once in, things still didn't feel quite right, as quickly became apparent on the first few trips down the learner's slope.

What's worse than being a double amputee? Being a double amputee who skis badly after a life of skiing quite well. Those first few tentative runs were very depressing, resulting in the tradesman blaming his tools. But it wasn't the boots that were the problem at all, well not after a bit of cutting here and packing there, but the leg sockets themselves. Whenever I initiated a turn, the mind worked, the upper body worked, and the stumps turned in the sockets — very disconcerting, somewhat painful and potentially extremely damaging. Without the services of knowledgeable people I tried to fix the situation myself. I tried things like putting on so many socks and so much packing around my stumps that it brought tears to my eyes trying to stuff them into the sockets. Once I tried lubricating the stump and socket liner with motor oil

(I didn't have Vaseline or talc on the field at the time) so I could cram them in extra tight. The result was very sore stumps with all the blood squeezed out of them and no improvement in my skiing. A few goes at that sort of thing with little improvement turned me off skiing for a while — not off the idea, just the doing of it.

It wasn't until early in 1990 on my first big OE, in Utah, that I got the skiing bug again and the tools to do it well. I was in Park City, Utah, for a medical conference, presenting some work I had done in the Haematology Research Unit at the Christchurch School of Medicine. What a conference, they certainly know how to conduct business in winter there. Every morning the conference would start at 7 am with breakfast meetings and presentations. These would continue to about 9.30 or 10 am. Then everyone would head for the slopes, slopes that rate at the top of all North American ski fields. These are the same slopes that hosted the 2002 Winter Olympics and Paralympics. Well, left stranded in a ski town can be somewhat frustrating, especially when one of the chairlifts goes right over the main street and there is a snow base of 11 feet. Wandering around the base facilities I came across the American Vietnam Veterans Administration Disabled Skiing Centre, a huge building, as big as most New Zealand ski lodges. Walking in the door I knew I was in the right place: legs and arms lying around, wheelchairs and mono skis everywhere.

After explaining my situation, we sat down and went through what would be needed to get me up and skiing again. Basically a new set of legs especially designed to handle the forces of skiing, with thigh straps and knee braces to maintain control without damaging the stumps. A ski guide/instructor was appointed to show me around the mountain the following day after setting me up with some temporary soft-style knee braces, a bit like overgrown ankle bandages, and some skis. The gondola trip to almost 10,000 feet was enough to get the head spinning for a start, and standing at the top of a ski run was a bit surreal. My first decent ski run in eight years and it was 4000 vertical feet! After the first few turns I knew two things for certain: it was achievable, I would really be able to do it; and it was a bloody long way down. Every turn was done with real care, I was too far from home to stuff a stump, and the thought of American medical costs was scary for a Kiwi on his first big OE.

What a buzz! Forget science, I was skiing again. And while it was pretty tentative, I could see the potential with a decent set of ski legs. Once back down at the base lodge I started photographing the ski legs of a single-amputee instructor, determined to get a set designed and built once back home in Christchurch. The staff there laughed, the legs I was photographing were copies of the best ski legs around — those made in my own limb centre in Christchurch. I'm sure they had been holding out on me for years to save a bit of tax-payers' money, as, unlike today, we could generally get two sets of legs at a time compliments of the government.

So there I was, knocking on the door of the Limb Centre as soon as I arrived back on the tarmac at Christchurch, ringing the local branch of Disabled Skiing, and planning my next obsession, skiing.

'Disabled Skiing', just the name had always had the connotations of 'gimp' to me, the impression that they were there to make a few disabled people feel good. How wrong I was. What I encountered was an organisation that took people and gave them tools for growth. It was an organisation that operated on several levels, from just giving people a buzz, a new experience, to challenging them, taking them out of their comfort zone, and on to the training of elite athletes. It was the first time I had come upon elite disabled athletes, world champions and medal winners in sports that weren't just there to be participated in but won.

The trick was how to afford it when struggling with a young family, having just finished university, holding a modestly paid job and the inevitable mortgage. It was like so many other things before and yet to come in my life that I had either left too late or didn't necessarily have the focus to become totally involved in. In fact that's a component of disabled sport that many forget or don't realise — quite often the participants are somewhat older because by the time they have had their accidents or illnesses, recovered or rehabilitated, and then got around to involving sport in their lives again, years have often slipped by.

The Canterbury disabled skiing group gave me the tools to get involved again. Instruction, subsidised travel and tickets all made the sport, the latest obsession, that much more achievable.

Still wasn't easy though, not on the family, or me, especially when I'd head off in the van with the others. Knowing that we could afford one to ski, but not everyone to ski, was difficult. Just like some of those early years at Mount Cook, I'd feel guilty (for a damn good reason) for 'having fun' or at least being perceived to be having it. I didn't see it that way though. Sure I had fun, but more importantly for me, I was pushing myself, challenging myself and growing with it, growing what I saw as opportunities for the family, for our future growth. The reality was, I guess, that I was using up valuable family cash, cash we didn't have at the time.

Every day that I skied in 1990 I became more and more certain I would be able to race to the highest level in the world. The National Champs at Mount Hutt that year, where I won silver medals in the Slalom and Giant Slalom, were proof to me that I was getting there. Actually they were like a consolation prize for trying hard but being nowhere near the level needed. Everyone I spoke to congratulated me on how well I was doing. 'Great,' I thought, 'I'm on the way.'

There was no way I could afford either the time off work or the cost to spend the 1990–91 northern hemisphere season at the mecca of disabled skiing, Winter Park, Colorado. The New Zealand team, which I dreamt of joining, spent six to eight weeks there training and racing. Back home in New Zealand I was trying to ski twice a week during the rest of the 1990 winter, on Wednesdays and Sundays, both days with the Disabled Skiing group. This meant working Saturdays and any other day I didn't ski, to try and keep up with the research workload at the clinical school. Come summer and I was out on my mountain bike starting to get some base fitness for the following winter.

It was during that summer that I was involved in the Bank of New Zealand's Achiever's Programme. An advertisement for each of the achievers was filmed, mine focusing on the science, skiing and the mountain bike. The advert finished with me pulling into the clinical school bike stands and heading up to my lab. Well, the advert worked very well, my bike was stolen the day after it showed on television. Obviously bike thieves in Christchurch who watched television now knew where there was a great mountain bike for the taking, whose owner wouldn't be able to catch them, even if they biked slowly. The small fee for the advert certainly didn't cover the cost of a new bike.

I needed skis and decent boots to go further, as I had learnt very quickly that it was still important to have good boots even though I had artificial feet — in fact it was even more important than if I had real feet. Not because of comfort but because of the dynamic action good boots can give you, making up for not having an ankle that you can control. I was sponsored into a pair of boots half way through one season, but I had to give them back because while they were top-level boots they didn't have the exact characteristics to help me replace that ankle. The boots I found that did work were, of course, the most expensive around, over $600 in early 1991. As luck would have it there was a pair of these Raichle Super Comp boots for sale, but only in a men's size 6. Well that was easy to fix: with a sharp knife I went from being my old standard 8½ to size 6 right there in the shop. Best move I ever made — both the boots, which worked fine, and the change in foot size — there are always size 6 men's shoes on sale, always a bargain around. But skis were more expensive, the Atomic importers at the time, Ski Industries in Christchurch, kindly gave an untried and untested gimp a 'pro' deal, more affordable, but just the beginning of a large Visa bill that hung over our heads for years.

To ski seriously in that winter of 1991, I really needed to do two things. First, to train for a period of three or more weeks at Cardrona, near Wanaka, with the New Zealand and US disabled ski teams, and then join them on a South Pacific ski race series. To fund the training and competition I arranged some sponsorship to help cover some costs, from a new tavern and restaurant in Christchurch, the Pegasus Arms, and a clothing company, Snoclothes.

The Limb Centre and I played around with some leg technology at that time as well. I had some great walking legs, Seattle LightFoot, made of an advanced composite material based on nylon and plastics. These were energy storage legs, the more force you put into them the more spring you got back. It seemed like a great idea for skiing — increasing the dynamic movement of the legs and boots. But as with all new ideas this one had a small flaw, which I was to find out about at 9 am one morning. An important part of any ski training is the dangerous high speed work, travelling at speeds over 60 km per hour, and as high as 100 in some cases. You have no chance of avoiding other wayward skiers at those speeds, so we had access to Cardrona in the early mornings (7 am–9 am) before the public made it onto the field. Runs in the bitterly cold mornings were exhilarating, fighting the huge centrifugal forces while carving turns at high speed. Of course we saved the last run until the chairlifts were almost full of the day's skiers, using the pylons as race gates, skiting to the max. Half way down the double chair on one of those skiing runs I discovered the composite material gets seriously weakened with cold, as it snapped off just above the boot in the middle of a high speed turn. I must have somersaulted four or five times before coming to a halt on my back under the chair. People were screaming for the ski patrol, yelling at me, telling me to hold on — why all the fuss I just couldn't work out. In fact I was in the middle of a ski-pole-banging tantrum because I had just snapped my only set of legs and I would have to walk 50 metres uphill to retrieve the leg with boot still attached. Looking up the slope I could see the ski stuck in the snow by its tail, a jagged white bone-like shaft sticking out of the boot. No wonder they all freaked out, thinking some poor sod had just snapped his leg off — and, actually, he had. Back to the drawing board and the substitution of sturdy aluminium in place of the composites.

It was near the end of that month of training at Cardrona that I got one of the biggest knocks to my psyche, had one of my greatest learning experiences, though I didn't necessarily know it then.

After a hard day's training, after almost four weeks of skiing nearly every day, we had a video training session. Training had been going all right, every one was telling me how well I was doing. A few told me how much better I needed to be, but I pretty much ignored them. Sitting back at the lodge that night for the video analysis we all had fun poking the borax at everyone's run. I saw one person skiing like a stick insect, all stiff, no angles, no dynamic action, virtually staggering down the slope. I laughed as much as everyone until I realised it was me, I was that pathetic-looking stick insect. I was absolutely shattered, and did what all Kiwi males do when confronted with that level of truth — I went and got thoroughly pissed.

The funny thing was I was furious at everyone who had told me I was doing great, people who were trying to buoy up my spirits to keep me interested in the sport and in going further. In fact, because they didn't understand me and the way I work, they had in effect told me time and time again that I didn't need to try harder, that I was doing fine. All this certainly took the wind out of my sails, destroyed what growing confidence I had, and that just inhibited me from learning. Pretty stuffed up all round really.

I went on that season to compete in the South Pacific ski race series, held at Mount Hotham in Australia and Cardrona. Teams and individuals from around the world were to come, no big numbers but some decent competition anyway. The races were real competition with all the stress of just competing added to the nerves generated by the challenge, and even fear, of real ski racing. I quickly realised that I just didn't have that killer mentality, even back then. Sure I did OK, with some bronze and silver medals, but at a great cost both in dollars and in personal stress. During every run I pictured myself as that disabled stick insect, not the elegant racer, reverse visualisation that had the expected effect of holding me back.

Home from the series, in debt by thousands of dollars, the family pissed off with me for being away so much and blowing the year's budget, with the aim of turning skiing into a future pretty much sunk. New Zealand wasn't big enough to support a professional disabled performance type of business, my dream, and I didn't have either the cash and assets or the imagination and confidence to pick up the whole

My first skiing medals (two silvers), 1990.

family and head to potentially greener pastures overseas.

In my absence, Anne had got our 'project' ex-state house, in the Christchurch suburb of Spreydon, painted with help from our parents, installed new kitchen appliances, and generally got on with life.

So what was I going to do? I felt frustrated at work: research was mostly fun but the funding for science sucked, especially if you needed to make money out of it, and the hours prohibited another job.

I was continually looking around for an interesting twist to my career in science, something that would allow me back into the fresh air but still stimulate the brain. Reading a Dick Francis novel re-awoke an interest in wine, the science and mystique of it, so when a job was advertised for a trainee winemaker for Montana in Blenheim, I was already primed for change.

I'm a strong believer that if you are mentally and emotionally ready for change, for new opportunity, then new directions and challenges almost seek you out. That advert asked for a person who had a good science degree, life experience and a love of wine — written for me, I was sure. An interview was granted, I suspect as much for curiosity and a chat about climbing with Andy Frost (senior winemaker) as for my qualifications.

As part of the interview process I needed to demonstrate an ability to move around the winery and undertake some of the winemaking tasks such as pulling hoses, climbing up and down the catwalk ladders, constantly being observed. Quite a chuckle I thought at the time.

I was thankful that I got that chance to change direction, especially entering the wine industry at such a pivotal time. Montana's share price was at an all-time low and the company was in the throes of re-inventing itself. Major international awards had just been won; it was the start of an era of dramatic growth.

Initially I was there as trainee winemaker. Montana was developing its prospective winemakers (and still does to a large extent) from people who had good science degrees and the desire to make and experience wine. Being a large commercial concern though, each winemaker needs to rely on an integrated team to make the final product, especially if

Gareth Eyres/*North & South*

Above: In the vineyard, the origin of all great wines; at Fairhall vineyard, vintage 2002.

Below: Presentation of a personalised six litre bottle of Deutz on my last day with Montana, May 2002.

Gareth Eyres/*North & South*

Left: The daily ride ritual: swapping walking legs for my Britten-designed riding legs.

Right: Feeling 'at home' in my office — my cockpit — doing the hard miles.

Gareth Eyres/*North & South*

A silver medal that felt better than gold: on the podium, Sydney, October 2000.

Top: From left, Spoon, Charlie, Narly and me on the Pukaki Boulder, December 2001.

Above: Legs for every occasion: two sets of riding legs on the left, skiing legs on the right and climbing legs at the front.

Right: Crevasse rescue and prussik practice on the Pukaki Boulder.

aiming to take on the world, as we were. It was and is in this aspect of winemaking that the 'life experience' part of the equation becomes essential. No use having a great desire to make wine and the skill to do it if no one will do as you want, because no matter how hard you try, you can't be there 24 hours a day doing everything yourself.

I actually evolved from trainee winemaker into the 'cellar master', essentially the foreman or day-to-day manager of the winery. I guess my life experience was such that I was not bad at handling people, inspiring them in a small way. After 18 months of that role though, I needed to get back to actively making wine, and moved into an assistant winemaker's role and then from there to a full winemaking position, all in the Marlborough winery. Fantastic times, especially the development of Deutz and the rieslings from Marlborough, wines that I had a real affinity with from day one at Montana.

The family stayed in Christchurch for the first three months of my new job while Anne sold the house and I helped look for a new one in Blenheim. We would meet at Hanmer Springs occasionally during that time, the start of a love affair with that magical little alpine township.

Work at Montana was always all-consuming, but that's just the nature of the wine industry. Vintage is the crux of the winegrowing and winemaking year, the time when the whole potential profit for the company comes in. The grapes represent the true potential of the resulting wines; they are the benchmark and everything a winemaker does from picking onwards (including the decision of when to pick) will either maintain and display that potential to the world or else diminish it. A difficult concept for people to grasp in many ways, as the result of any action (short of losing wine down the drain or some other accident) can only be seen months or years later, and frequently can never be quantified. Is that wine you are having with your dinner the best it could be, the true reflection of the grapes? You just never know, even the winemaker doesn't, that's part of the true challenge and hook that is winemaking. To do it well you need a driving passion — yes, it certainly helps if you are of the obsessive mould. If not, you are only making a beverage, not really worth the effort. The upshot is that you work a minimum of

Doing the rounds at Montana Wines, checking the red ferment tanks.

12 hours per day, seven days a week, for the whole harvest and generally the month after as well. In Marlborough that means from early March until late June, a long time to maintain your passion and be virtually separated from your non-work world. Winemakers' families may as well go on holiday for three months or so.

I needed a release from the intensity of winemaking and found it in skiing again in 1996. This time at least the family had some more involvement, probably not enough, but I was learning. With the annual New Zealand Disabled Ski Week and Championships scheduled for August, I decided that the planning of a trip combining the champs and some wine work for Montana in Queenstown and Wanaka would be just the ticket. Before I was game to head south though, I needed some time on the boards and a few lessons to resurrect what skill I had. The difference between 1991 and 1996 in how I approached skiing was due to a difference in my understanding of my disability and myself. Montana had utilised a team of corporate psychologists to help staff understand how they worked, the Human Synergistic team. Through the tools they gave me I finally understood how that situation in 1991 came about, and learnt to be far more aware of how other people view me and interact with me. Because I live within my disability I forget that people see me as Mark Inglis, Double Amputee, rather than just as Mark Inglis.

I took several lessons at the Rainbow Ski Resort (Nelson Lakes) in July that year and didn't let anyone know that I was an amputee. I did three runs with an instructor. After the first run he explained exactly what I was doing wrong and what to do to put it right. The second run, some fine tuning, and by the third run I was skiing better than I had done before I lost my legs. All you need is to get the right unbiased advice and work hard at implementing it and you're away. What a relief and a revelation. After several runs that day the instructor saw me tightening the ski leg suspension system and was blown away; he thought I was just a rusty intermediate or above skier. Rust was right though, both in the mind and the ski legs. The extra advice he gave me that day means I now ski with confidence most places and get better with every run.

August was a chance for me to show my old coach Pete McCallum that I could learn, that I could actually ski now I understood myself better. Skiing down the piste to meet Pete that first time after five years was one of the proudest moments of my life. I had a fantastic week skiing, did some races, and even managed to burgle gold in the Masters racing.

That confidence transferred directly into my everyday life, and that is the true power of organisations like Disabled Skiing in New Zealand, long may it thrive and send disabled/able people with that confidence back into the community. They won't just be a boon to themselves and other disabled, but their ability should be an inspiration to all.

7 SYDNEY 2000 PARALYMPICS: SO MANY ATHLETES, SO FEW LIMBS

JULY 2000, THE FIRST STAGE of the Tour de France. The tour always starts with a short time trial or 'prologue'. The newest and lowest ranked rider goes first, the previous year's winner (cancer survivor Lance Armstrong) goes last and all 175 other cyclists in this, the world's premier cycle race, go in between.

One of the first off is a young British rider, David Millar (riding for the French team, Cofidis). He puts in a scorching ride, at 19:03:11 the fastest time so far, but there are still 143 to ride. Millar, after riding at an average speed of over 51.9 kmh, is now in the position of having to wait for each of those 143, including most of the world's best cyclists, to ride before he will know his final placing.

The TV coverage follows the emotions and reactions of Millar as each rider comes in slightly slower than his time, each one increasing the tension and expectation in the team caravan. Millar can't decide whether to be glued to the monitors or hide his head; in fact he does both at various times. Finally, Number 1, the last rider, Lance Armstrong comes in . . . seconds slower. The pent-up emotion of David Millar bursts over the screen, his first tour and he has the *malliot jaune*, the yellow leader's jersey, one of the most prized trophies in cycling and world sport. On the first day he achieves the ultimate dream of every cyclist, but what a way to do it.

Whenever I replayed that prologue I thought, 'I hope that is never me.' The stress of watching each rider looked huge, especially when it came to the last few and the anticipation generated must have been unbelievable.

Well, on the 18th of October 2000, in the Dunc Grey Velodrome, Sydney, that really was me. Not 177 riders, just 17, but the best Paralympic cyclists in the world that year. I rode 10th out of the 17 and yep, David Millar's emotions were right on the button.

How do you get to the Paralympics? Well, as with my climbing, we need to go back a few years first, back to 1997.

I really have to thank Montana for rekindling my passion for cycling. Ever since those early days at Mount Cook when the mountain bike was a tool to get out and about, to get a bit extreme, I've ridden bikes, both mountain bikes and road riding. But it was a desire to get really fit again after skiing in 1996 that made me start riding my mountain bike seriously again. Then in August 1997 Montana sent me to California to work in the wine industry. With my technical research science background I had been working on some new technologies for our laboratories. Most wine labs rely on simple 'wet chemistry', which is basic and cheap to set up but doesn't have the ability to give detailed information about the components of grapes and wine. This wet chemistry is the sort of alchemy, or magic, that you used to do in the school lab, mixing various chemicals to get different colours that mean something to those who know the secrets. To move Montana to a new level I had done a comparison of two new instrumental techniques, which were limited at the time to only the best-funded and largest international wineries, and the best place to see them in action was California. Also we had an association with Maison Deutz (subsequently relabelled as Laetitia), a premium champagne-style winemaker Maison

Deutz and Montana were both closely associated with Deutz of Champagne. Christian Roguenau, the winemaker at Maison Deutz and a good friend, had just had taken delivery of a new-generation wine press similar to those at Montana. As I had significant expertise in setting up and running them, it was decided to lend me to Christian.

Ah, California. Sun, sun and more sun. Before heading to the US I had always hated the heat; I used to say, 'You can always put more clothes on when it gets too cold but there is only a finite number of clothes you can take off (without grossing people out) when it gets too hot.'

But California certainly changed that. Maison Deutz was near the coast, half way between Los Angeles in the south and San Francisco in the north. The area, based around the vibrant university city of San Luis Obispo, is (surprisingly) known as the Central Coast.

California is the home of the mountain bike; Marin County, north of San Francisco, is the birthplace of the bikes and the culture. After a few days there I knew I had to get a bike. You can't be there without riding, it's just not right. Christian kindly lent me his bike — bad move that, because that was about the last he saw of me. At each and every spare moment I would head out to the nearest wilderness area, Montana de Oro (Golden Mountain, because of the sand dunes but very appropriate). Riding the trails of the Central Coast was a real buzz, day by day I was getting fitter and lighter, revelling in the burningly hot but ultra-dry weather. The relief from the heat came in two forms: the ubiquitous air conditioning (cars, shops, bars, hotels, motels, malls, everywhere) and swimming pools.

Riding was always exciting with the wildlife there — saw my first snake, dead on the road. When I saw my first rattler all I could think as I retreated at a great rate of knots was, 'Glad I've got fibreglass ankles.' In Montana de Oro the signs warn bikers and walkers to keep to the tracks to avoid the attention of mountain lions. Back in New Zealand we had always thought Christian was pulling our collective leg when he told stories of mountain lions as vineyard pests, but in the short time I was there, three cases were reported of the big cats coming in to the edge of town, right into people's backyards.

I headed north from San Luis Obispo, driving over 3500 miles (5600 km), looking at how the wineries of the Napa and Sonoma operate and riding the trails and wilderness parks at every opportunity. Imagine riding in Jack London National Park, where *Call of the Wild* was written. The place just oozes history, there is an eerie feel to the ruins of his wilderness mansion, and the forest is dotted with 'Beware of the Rattlers' signs, ensuring everyone but the most adventurous stays on the trails.

The highlight of the time was Yosemite. The magical mix of riding the trails and being in a place that is almost sacred ground for a climber was inspirational to say the least. I spent two days hammering the trails to all the big walls, climbs that I knew off by heart, as intimately as though I'd climbed them myself. It was my first visit to the valley, but I was brought up on the stories of Royal Robbins and the other pioneers of big wall climbing. A lot of my friends had made the pilgrimage to climb at Yosemite over the years, some who are still around, others who are not.

Stump health in the hot weather was a continuing battle, especially when riding. Think of it as wearing gumboots 18 hours a day when the average daytime temperature is above 35°C. Regular sock changes, lots of stump washing in cold clean water was the daily routine. At the start of the trip I was really only able to ride for 30 minutes without getting blistered stumps or ripped skin, but by the end of the trip it was nearer a hard 90 minutes on the bike.

I came back to New Zealand after five weeks away, ready to fire; begged the loan of a road bike and started to do some miles.

Obsessed? Perhaps. Passionate? Definitely.

But where to from here? Racing seemed the natural progression, more as a challenge to myself and a display of ability than anything else. I tried a couple of mountain bike races, but they were very frustrating because the terrain involved regular bike carries. Why, when you have a bike race, would you want to carry your bike? It's a *bike* race for god's sake. Any chance of being competitive went out the window with the first carry. It was a bank five metres high with a track just 20 cm wide (bloody narrow with a bike on your shoulder) sidling across it near the top. As well as carrying the bike you needed balance and careful foot placement — well that wasn't going to happen. The organisers kindly offered an alternative route for me, but if I did that then I wouldn't be in the race, at least to my mind anyway.

While at the Limb Centre shortly afterwards, I wandered over to the offices of Parafed Canterbury. Both are in the grounds of Burwood Hospital, my old 'home'. I had always been aware Parafed existed but, like many, always thought that they were really only interested in wheelchair sport. I couldn't have been more wrong. Graham Condon, Ken Sowden and Ben Lucas immediately gave me wads of information on Paralympic cycling, new in New Zealand but a strong sport overseas, especially in Europe, America and Australia. It was through the guidance and inspiration of Ben Lucas that I was able to fashion my newly kindled passion for cycling into a focused sport, an outlet for my need for change, my need for a new challenge.

It was at this stage in late 1997 that I hooked up with Wayne Alexander and his innovative legs, which added more fuel to the fire. I was hanging around the Parafed office one day, when Ben asked if I would be keen to talk to Wayne at Britten Motorcycles about a scheme he had to make some sports legs. Well, ask any Kiwi male if he wants to peek inside the Britten factory and he would probably offer you his first-born for the chance. They were offering me not just the chance to look inside that place where legends and dreams are made, but to become the 'test pilot'.

At the time Wayne was looking into new innovations for the research and engineering side of the Britten company. He had also been with the Britten race team for two years, had built the last two bikes and ran the workshop. He had been a friend of John Britten's from the early days, and was associated with a lot of the wide-ranging projects John had on the go. The leg concept was all about creating an innovative new style of sports leg, one that performed well but was also going to be able to be mass-produced cheaply. There are plenty of great legs around, but 99 per cent of the world's amputees can not afford them, with many not being able to afford legs at all. The first prototypes Wayne produced had a polymer ankle joint, the aim being to replicate the real ankle, in movement if not in looks. Imagine my surprise when I saw those limbs, built out of panel steel (the stuff a car is made of), brazed together and sitting on the bench of the workshop. For me it was a real dilemma, what to look at first, one of two Britten V1000s sitting there, the orginal 'Cardinal' Britten or these agricultural twin spar legs that looked as if they were heavy enough to anchor a boat.

After dragging my eyes away from the bikes we started work on the legs. Right from our very first discussions we knew that we would be wasting our time making the stump sockets when the limb centre staff had years of experience and loads of expertise. Therefore the first job in leg testing was dismantling an old set of legs and using the sockets bolted directly on the new lower leg/ankle. Even the foot was crafted out of panel steel, a work of art with a rubber sole attached, no shoes necessary.

After two steps I wanted to run and jump. I could tell that Wayne, with his lateral thinking, had come up with a great concept. The idea was to make something that could be cast out of light cheap components, and even with the first of these agricultural art works it was clearly going to be a winner.

But running wasn't what was exciting me at the time, it was how to cycle better and faster. Wayne had been involved in extreme sports such as the Southern Traverse Multi-Sport Race, both in competing and in providing teams with toys so they could go further and faster, so he had some definite ideas on how he could improve my cycling. Parallel to the ankle project, we played around with an old set of my legs, moving the foot position to maximise the power transmission. The trouble is, when you go out to ride and your legs and feet go around in circles, bits move. In fact, to be a great cyclist it takes years to train your body to perform the most efficient and powerful movements automatically. Try it, get on a bike, preferably with cycling shoes and 'clipless' pedals and pedal. Even better, ride beside a professional and watch. As the foot goes around, the toe goes from being level with the heel to a toe-down attitude, every stroke. My artificial limbs stayed fixed though, meaning

I looked like a waddling duck when trying to pedal. With the world champs looming we weren't going to be able to make a moving ankle, and although Wayne knew what he wanted, the 'test pilot' wasn't quite so sure. As an interim, he butchered an old set of legs, stripping off the cosmetic covers to lighten them and improve the aerodynamics. Most importantly he modified the ankle to put the foot at about a 15° downward tilt, towards the toe. The difference was miraculous, it instantly changed the way I rode — definitely an ugly-duckling-into-swan scenario, though it didn't make my butt any smaller.

With the legs strapped on, training started in earnest, with the Paralympic World Cycling Championships due to be held in September 1998. The reality was that from a base of virtually nothing I had set myself the task of getting a top 10 placing in Colorado Springs in six months' time. Unfortunately, three of those months would be the vintage, and I would be working over 12 hours per day, seven days a week, but that's winemaking.

I worked from about 11 am to after midnight each day, so to train I would ride to work in the mornings (minimum of 20 km and up to 50 km some days) and home again in the early hours of the morning. A saving grace was that at that hour of night there wasn't much traffic around to use me as target practice.

I used my knowledge of physiology to design a plan to try and get myself up to standard before September, but there are no shortcuts in cycling (except cheating with drugs, far too prevalent), just the miles and hours on the road. But even I recognised that I couldn't do it all myself, what I needed was someone's experience to tap into, a coach. I asked around, people I respected in the bike world, and they all said go and see Tony Catterick, he knows what he's on about and you'll get on great. Being a bit rebellious by nature, the last thing I wanted was a little Hitler or a rigid thinker. The coach had to look at me and see both the advantages and disadvantages in having a legless cyclist to train, and that's what I got with Tony, a healthy dose of realism. It was obvious just from the lack of miles in my legs that I wasn't going to set the world on fire in September, but we came up with an achievable plan to go and learn, to do my best, and come away smarter and stronger.

Montana came to my rescue again when it came to getting to the US. I was to be one of five Montana staff to launch our brand Brancott Vineyards into the US market during September and early October 1998. I was able to set aside 10 days in the middle of the trip to escape from New York and the East Coast and compete at Colorado Springs. Unfortunately it wasn't quite as straightforward as that, as Colorado Springs is 6000 feet above sea level, and the road race course even higher at 7400 feet. Doesn't sound high, doesn't feel particularly high, until you need to push your body to the limit, to the max. Then it hurts. Your body just can't get enough oxygen from the thin air at altitude until it has been there long enough to compensate. The science behind operating at altitude is really the basis for a lot of modern training techniques (and drugs) and hinges around the transport of oxygen (O_2) to the tissues by the red blood cells and their oxygen-carrying haemoglobin. When the available O_2 in the air drops (which is what happens at altitude) our bodies respond by increasing the production of the hormone erythropoetin, or EPO. This in turn increases the production of red blood cells. The concentration of red blood cells (RBC) at any one time in our blood is measured by our haematocrit, giving a percentage RBC number. An average athlete would be about 40 to 43 per cent, but after training at altitude for longer than two weeks the haematocrit would rise to close to 50 per cent. In cycling, if your haematocrit is above the magic 50 per cent you cannot (are not allowed to) race until it lowers. High levels of RBC, while carting heaps of O_2 around the body, also make the blood quite viscous, so thick to pump around that it can actually cause strokes, so it is one of the parameters measured in cycling during drug testing. At the Tour de France, riders are regularly measured in the mornings before riding, if over 50 per cent you're out.

It is this mechanism that is abused in various ways by drug cheats, who either inject themselves with artificial or animal EPO to get the haematocrit to rise, or who use artificial 'haem' to carry extra O_2.

When adapting to altitude it takes the body about nine days to produce more EPO and more RBC naturally. During the first three or four days you go downhill, each day worse than the one before, dropping probably 20 per cent of your performance potential. Then things start to get better, until after about nine days your body is performing at near enough to its pre-altitude level. Mind you, if you then go back down to sea level with your high haematocrit, it's like having an engine in your legs for at least three weeks.

Back to Colorado. Due to work constraints I had five days, just enough to hit rock bottom then start to come back up. Most teams (the New Zealand 'team' was three of us — no manager, mechanic, masseur, etc, just three athletes) were there for at least two weeks prior to racing, so were well acclimatised, but as I was there to learn I couldn't really justify the extra time.

Day 6 and the road race was first up, three laps of a 17-km circuit with a big hill in it, all between 6300 feet and 7400 feet. In the days beforehand as I was trying to acclimatise I barely made it up the hill. On one training ride, when I was at the bottom of the main climb I could see a small object in the distance high up the hill. When I finally got nearer I saw it was a bus — that's how big the hill was. The race really hurt, though during the first 3 km I thought, 'Great, I can do this,' then when we hit the hill and the 'hammer went down', the real race started. My heart rate had set a new maximum by three-quarters of the way up that hill; I dropped from the leading bunch, then from the second group. By the third and final lap I had made a few places up; of the 20 starters there were 16 left I think. The final hill before the finish line and I had one of the French in my slightly blurred sights, and the last 100 metres was a sprint by two very stuffed but intensely determined riders. Just pipped him for twelth in the race, a good result but not in the top 10 as I had planned and hoped.

Next came the road time trial, 16 km of rolling highway, on my ninth day at Colorado Springs. I'd stopped trying to cough up my lungs, had recovered pretty well from the earlier race and had a lot more respect for both the altitude and my fellow competitors. A good race, just on 28 minutes so not blistering but good enough for ninth in the world — I'd got my top 10.

I learnt so much: about preparation, training, the level required to do well and especially how to handle the bureaucracy involved in that level of sport. With no manager or team leader it seemed to fall to me to ensure all the i's were dotted and the t's crossed. Certainly an added stress when you should be focusing on doing your best.

At those world champs Paul Jesson of Christchurch showed his international class and commitment by winning the coveted World Champion's Jersey for the 4000-metre individual pursuit, probably one of the hardest cycling disciplines to master.

Travelling with bikes is never easy. Apart from the continual hassle of being overweight, just the bulk of two bike bags, wheel bags and your own luggage makes it difficult to move through airports. Add the complication of being a 'double amp' with spare legs as well and you need to give yourself plenty of time. I set off every airport gate security check X-ray alarm without fail. There's just enough titanium and stainless steel in the legs to make those bells ring. Most places you get taken aside and checked with the 'wand', but in LA and New York I was regularly put up against the wall and comprehensively frisked. I mostly wear shorts when travelling for that very reason; it makes life so much simpler if they know what they're dealing with. The up-side for me though is that if I get a spare seat I can lie right down, minus legs of course. On long haul flights (over three hours) I always spend over half the time with my legs off, either with a pillow on them to turn the 'cattle class' seat into a lazy-boy or tucked away under the seat with my stumps in the pocket of the seatback in front of me. Business or first class would be nicer of course, but you make the best of what you've got.

Travelling around the US with all that gear got a bit much, especially as every time I checked onto a United Airlines flight they would ask, 'Is that a bike, sir?' An innocent 'yes' always brought an automatic US$50 fee. Now with something like 10 internal flights it was going to get very expensive. To add insult to injury I was always over the baggage weight limit, another fee, but one that I had more success at talking my way out of. It all got a bit much in New York one day though, so out came the tools and the lower part of the cycling limbs went into the nearest trash can. I think it just about broke Wayne's heart when I told him (quite some time later and over the phone, that's for sure).

Back in New Zealand and back on the bike, I raced locally, as I still do occasionally, more to show my face for sponsors and to have someone to ride with than the desire for competition. I still needed legs to ride as those early 'jury-rigged' efforts spoilt me for riding with my walking legs.

Wayne used his incredible skill with carbon fibre (the heart of the Britten V1000 bikes) to provide me with a set of aerodynamic twin spar legs with the new ankle and toe alignment. These were done in beautiful black carbon fibre mat, the twin spars shaped like wings or aerofoils to cut through the air and weighing virtually nothing. The pedal cleat bolted directly onto the 'foot', meaning no expensive cycling shoes and even less rotating weight. The first race with these on had everyone stopping to look, all complaining that I now had an aerodynamic advantage.

The only international competition I was able to get to in 1999 was the Southern Cross Multidisability Games in Sydney. These were promoted as a trial run for the Paralympics, and while the road race course was essentially the same, the other cycling events were at old facilities around Sydney. I raced three events, a time trial and criterium on a rough winding suburban cycle track and the road race in Centennial Park near the centre of the city. I 'blew' in the time trial, that is I went too hard at the start so by two-thirds of the way through my legs went to jelly and my vision started to spin. I crept home in third place, unfortunately it was third of only four. LC3 riders were thin on the ground at that event. (LC3 is my class in racing so everyone has similar power, mostly single above knee amputees, a few double's like me and the occasional other broken body.)

The criterium (a short, tight circuit race) which followed had its moments as well. I was in a great position coming onto the last straight when I was naïve enough to get shunted onto the grass by someone with more racing experience than me. Back on the track, 150 metres to go, third looming again, then I thought 'bugger this' and hammered like never before. I went over the line in second, missing out on gold by half a wheel.

The road race was more of the same, more tactics, more having to read the race, but the best thing for me was that it had a hill. Not a big one, just 30 or 40 metres high, but enough. I had learnt my lesson in Colorado in 1998. Sounds dumb I know, but as a double amputee I have an advantage in sprinting and climbing purely because I can get out of the saddle. Most of my international competitors in the LC3 class are single above-knee amputees. Only one leg, but frequently a huge one. Having that one knee and lower limb means they are very strong in the saddle, great at time trialling and pursuiting, but they generally can't get out of the saddle. I'd seen this in Colorado, seen the potential strength and advantage I could have on a hilly course, and trained for it. Hours and hours were spent on the hills around Marlborough and they all paid off. The road race wasn't without controversy though. Early on in the race Paul Jesson and a Japanese rider had been dropped on the hill and they decided to just cruise the rest of the race leaving only two of us to battle it out on the hill each lap. Paul joined us for the last lap and decided to ride on the front, drafting us to the final uphill sprint at the finish line. (Drafting in cycling means getting behind the person in front. This means almost 30 per cent less energy expended for those following, meaning they have more energy left to sprint when it matters.) The only problem was I was on his wheel and the Australian, Noel Sens, was on mine — the worst situation I could think of. Paul pulled off the course just as the road started to head up, and I had no choice but to try to stall Noel and then sprint him off which, to my relief, was exactly how it happened. (Being in the front just before the finish is the worst position as you are in the wind and the person behind can leap frog in front of you, winning.)

My first international win, I was ecstatic. During the sprint I had felt so powerful, out of the corner of my eye I could see Noel drifting back as my two strengths, sprinting and hills, worked a treat. Lying under a tree with the other Kiwis I was feeling a buzz that approached the buzz of climbing, that feeling of putting everything on the line, doing something bloody hard and succeeding. It didn't last long though; while we were soaking up the sun the Australians put in a protest, they claimed that Paul had helped me win. A commissar came over and formally told me I was disqualified, I was no longer eligible for the medal even though I had won. I was furious, Paul had actually made my race much harder, he had put me in the worst position in cycling, in front at the start of a sprint. Luckily Wayne, the team manager, had years of experience in dealing with these situations. To get my medal back though, we had to write an appeal, then I had to appear before a judging panel of three race stewards. Luckily they were all ex-racers and could clearly see I had won in spite of the position Paul had inadvertently put me in, not because of it.

It was at that race that I realised that the Paralympics were a realistic goal for me. I had always said no use going, no sense making the sacrifices necessary, unless you think you're going to win. Not everyone thought I had a chance though; most commonly (and more so now) it was, 'Aren't you too old?' to which the reply must be, 'You're never too old.'

To get there from New Zealand was never going to be easy or particularly fair. There were always three athletes in the running for one place; then closer to the time, a second place became available when a wild card entry was given to New Zealand. The three of us had trained and competed together for the last three years: Paul Jesson, the world pursuit champ; Steve Maitland; and myself. We were the team from the 1998 Worlds and the 1999 Sydney Games. Paul and I were both in the LC3 class, Steve in the LC2, a class for single below-knee amputees. How do you choose between people of different classes, different disabilities (actually abilities), especially when our international competition is limited?

Well Paralympics New Zealand had that job, and recruited Cycling New Zealand selectors to help. The decision was based on our limited international performances and an assessment of each athlete including an interview. But as we all knew, the real way to get there (which we were all doing) was doing the miles, doing the hours and committing a large chunk of our lives (and those of our families) to the attempt.

Among the biggest hurdles was how I was going to afford to compete, and how I could be sure that I had the correct technical advice to maximise the little power that I had. Wayne had been great with the mechanics of the limbs, but what I really needed was professional cycling advice on how to get the muscles' power to the legs. So many people give so much advice that it can be pretty hard to sort through it all, and being a sceptic know-it-all doesn't help either. The only way I was going to be happy was to go to Sydney, to Steve Hogg's CycleFit business. So, using some of my Parafed and Paralympic training grants, I was able to get to Sydney in late 1999.

Cycling is such an intense repetitive action sport that any small fault in the way you pedal or sit can bring on overuse injuries very quickly and rob you of power, wasting all those hours of training. Steve had built a reputation for setting up all types of cyclists from weekend warriors to European professionals. One look at me and he thought he had a challenge, but in reality, because of all the work Wayne and I had already done, the two-hour consultation was done in less than an hour, with only minimal changes to me or the bike. Extremely valuable though was the revelation that my left leg was putting out less force than my right. Some on-the-spot re-engineering of the left leg helped to alleviate the problem to some extent, well worth the trip. Steve was as enthusiastic as Wayne, waiving the normal fee. It was a long way to go to get advice that perhaps I could have got somewhere in New Zealand, but when it comes from someone with the credentials of Steve it adds real confidence and power to the psyche as well as the legs.

Money was still a problem; a new bike for the road could cost as much as $10,000, certainly more than $5000. A track bike was also needed (anywhere from $3000 to $14,000) and Wayne had new ideas for some legs. I sought advice from Ben Lucas at Parafed who suggested I apply for an AMP Scholarship, the closing date for which was only five days away. A quick surf of the Internet yielded the application form, surprisingly only two pages. 'Well,' I thought, 'it's not going to take long to fill this in.' In fact they gave you so little room to write that you had to make sure every word counted. Basically I appealed to them to help me achieve my dream, a combination of getting the resources to compete at the Paralympics on an even field with other athletes from around the world, and also to continue the development of the legs with Wayne with the aim that one day we would have sport limbs readily available, or at least make people aware of the options for amputees.

I must have hit a chord, I guess, because that first application has developed into an association that has lasted three years now. That first interview was scary, more like a job interview really, with three leaders of AMP, including John Drabble, then the CEO of AMP in New Zealand. From the very first contact with Jon Slack, the scholarship manager (now in the UK), I was impressed with the professional tenor of the place.

'These people really want to help people achieve their dreams,' was my first thought. It was great to see that the whole company seemed to have ownership of the idea, they certainly weren't just paying lip service to an ad campaign. That first year (1999/2000) I was awarded one of twelve $3000 scholarships, then shortly after I also gained one of only two $20,000 scholarships that year. The money was split between bikes, wheels, training costs and legs (not as much as Wayne would have liked or probably deserved). What the scholarship did was give me the tools I needed, removing some of the constraints, or, as I said at the time, removing excuses for not performing on the day. Much of the money found its way to Scotty Brown's CycleSave in Christchurch, Scotty supporting me by getting the best deals around and just being the totally enthusiastic, mad bugger that he is.

While the dollars helped at one level, they also created an expectation for me that I would be good enough to go to Sydney. As I explained earlier, that decision was by no means certain. AMP had made it clear that even if I didn't get selected, the scholarship was all about helping me on the journey, and did not come with an expectation of success on their part — but there was definitely one on my part.

Montana was full steam ahead as always, and going into vintage that year with what I had just loaded up on my shoulders gave me the shivers, but as always I am forever cursed or blessed with total self-confidence, 'Course I can do it.'

For me the timing of the selection process was pretty traumatic. By half way through vintage I remember sitting down with Andy Frost, my boss, and saying, 'Well that's it, vintage has stuffed any chance of me being fit enough for the selection.' I was pissed off, tired, and sick of the continual juggle of work, family and training. Working an extremely intense 12–15 hours a day, seven days a week for about 10 weeks, and trying to train for an hour to an hour and a half a day as well just doesn't work without something breaking. Basically when you pile that much on yourself something has to give. You just have to hope that it's not your family, your career or your health. The reality of working and training at that level is that all four (including your performance) are affected.

It's at this time a coach, a mentor, becomes essential. Every year I've been involved in cycling I've learnt the value of having a coach just a bit more, especially once you enter the elite envelope of performance. I'm a bit of a know-it-all, always have been (as most people will tell you), but while I have the technical data (I've researched nutrition, physiology, sport-specific training and everything else to death), you still really need that true coach.

Luckily for me, I had Tony Catterick as coach and mentor and while his role for 2000 had a lot to do with saying 'calm down', 'take a rest day'or 'go easy' when I needed it, because for some of us going hard is never a problem, he was also careful to help me manage my programme to put me in the best position, not easy for either of us but essential if you want to succeed. I feel as guilty as hell having a day off. He was the person to say 'you look terrible', 'you look great', 'why are you doing that?', 'how will that get you on the podium?' For me Tony has been, and still is, a great mirror, a devil's advocate, and I have had the privilege of being able to tap into his experience, to try and avoid all the classic mistakes.

Unlike a lot of the other Paralympic athletes I didn't go overseas to compete and train prior to the 2000 Paralympics. I tend to work best in my home environment, staying focused and using every hour to the max. I didn't (and still don't) believe that I needed to go to Europe to race others in my disability class; if I needed racing there was always someone faster than me here in Marlborough or Nelson every Saturday, not 24 hours of flying and disruption away. Here at home I had access to Tony's expertise every day, something you shouldn't undervalue.

And it works: given the commitment, time and planning, you can do anything.

Even feeling really low post vintage, I continued building. I had set out a plan with Tony that we thought would get me to a top international standard and I was determined to stick with it. As work became more sane, the hours on the bike went up. In the two months prior to Sydney, I was spending 14–20 hours a week on the bike and in the gym. In addition I was spending about six to eight hours a day at work — sometimes you just don't know when to let go. The family hardly saw me and when they did I wasn't necessarily pleasant — hard on all of us.

Sitting at my desk late one evening in May 2000, I got the dreaded phone call from Dave Currie, the Chef de Mission for the 2000 Games. Luckily he came right out with congratulations, because I would have fainted from oxygen deprivation if they had mucked around, I couldn't breathe until I knew one way or the other. The first thought was pretty vocal, a huge YES, the second thought was for Steve, just gutted that someone had to miss out. Sport can be a real bugger at times. I guess we all knew from the outset that Paul, as world champ, had to be a certain pick, so the choice for the selectors was always going to be between Steve and myself.

If you ever need motivation, then being selected to represent your country dumps it onto you in bags.

The following months were a whirlwind of training, eating and sleeping, with some work and family thrown in. It was only in the last few weeks that I stayed away from work completely. Montana was fantastic, letting me deal with a lot of my workload from home by email and working afternoons and evenings so I could train and recover in the mornings.

In July AMP approached me to make one of their television commercials (TVC), an obligation that came with the scholarship. That was really fun, Dennis and Declan, Duster and Pete, the guys that had the job of designing and making the TVC, created a fun advert, partly because the crew had real life to them. The filming took four days, with one day on Mount Hutt skiing. Now while I love skiing, I hadn't skied for three years, so it wasn't just the ski legs that were rusty; I wasn't sure if the brain would remember the lessons learnt at Rainbow in 1996 and 1997. Of even more concern, as Tony reminded me, was how pissed off I would be if I did myself some damage while on skis. I agreed to the filming on the basis that I would only do the few runs necessary to get the minimum useable footage for the TVC. But as usual the brain had little say in the end, as by the time I had done a run to loosen up the rust, the skiing bug had bitten hard and I skied the whole day, fantastic fun and injury-free luckily. It is pretty hard to hurt yourself with the bionic ski legs I wear, they have enough leather, metal and carbon fibre in them to do serious damage to anyone else other than me. Filming finished with some taping of Wayne at work and some house shots. That's where the stunt doubles come in, as the family calls them, no, not people, but the mail box and house we borrowed near Christchurch for filming (easier than taking the whole crew to Renwick).

Winter training is never easy, cold mornings and wet days, though luckily for me in Marlborough the cold mornings generally gave way to sunny mild days and rain was rare with our droughts. Tony devised some killer workouts: 'train harder than you race' echoed in my inner ear while I hammered up killer hills or did the dreaded one minute thirty repetitions to simulate the kilo I was to ride at Sydney.

I came close to blowing all my hard work though, when testosterone took over from brains in the Glenhope to Murchison race. An ideal finish to months of training and a way to gauge my form, this is a 40-km race over rolling terrain beside the Buller River, and is always well patronised by cyclists in the top half of the South Island. A dismal day, with showers and a cold wind for Jeremy (16 years old and kicking my arse on the bike) and me, competing together. We went off with the second fastest group, I felt great — pulled to the front with Jeremy, made plenty of people hurt, put in some good climbs at the front of the pack, so I knew I was on track for Sydney. Tony had told me, 'Stay out of trouble, especially near the end as there will be a lot of inexperienced people going fast.' But as I was riding so well, I put the hammer down a kilometre from the finish, thinking, 'Oh well, get out in front of them, by far the best place to keep out of trouble.' But within 500 metres of the finish line they came thundering past; somebody's handlebar hooked mine and down I went. It happened so fast, before I knew it my head had hit the tarseal and I was tumbling down the road legless. As I watched my $11,000 Bianchi bike (with my legs still attached) heading for a fence I was thinking 'don't break, don't break'. When everything stopped moving I was sitting in the middle of the highway in the pouring rain and all I could smell was sheep shit — a stock truck had just been through. Cars were bearing down on me so I crawled to the road edge rapidly becoming aware that I had lost a lot of skin all over. Most worrying was my stumps; both had all the skin scraped off the top of the knee and a few patches the size of 50 cent pieces missing from near the end of the stump and the residual tibia (front, to you). A Nelson family kindly stopped and retrieved my legs and found my socks for me.

I have learnt the hard way over the years to get the stumps straight back into the sockets after an accident to prevent swelling. If you don't, it can be days before you can squeeze them on again — very unpleasant. Once upright and all limbs moving, the damage assessment started. The bike first of course: smashed left STI lever (very expensive), bent derailleur hanger (luckily replaceable), but frame not bent, so relatively lucky. The legs had left a lot of carbon fibre on the road and would need some patches but not too bad. Less good was the body, when I got to it. Large bits of skin missing from thighs, butt, fingers, wrists and elbows. When I lifted the flap of skin on the elbow you could see bone: 'May need the odd stitch,' I thought.

I got back on and finished the race, the fall and recovery had only taken 10 minutes, so my 40 km time was 1:11 I think, instead of 1:01.

Unfortunately Jeremy and I had planned on riding back to the car as Anne and the girls weren't due for a few hours, another 40 km after the race, a good warm down. The ride back though quickly became a no go as a bit of shock and cold rain settled in and the bruising started to make itself felt. Within 15 minutes I was stiff and freezing. Instead we sat beside a fire at the local cafe while the prizegiving was on, me dripping blood everywhere from my elbow and my clothing started to stick to the huge raw patches. I'd tried the local hospital but there was no one home. Anne arrived after an hour and we made our way on the 130 km home, then straight into the emergency department at Wairau Hospital. The real concern for me was the risk of infection from all the gravel embedded in my hide, especially as it had been marinated in sheep shit. Two and a half hours of scrubbing and stitching, some anti-inflammatories, antibiotics and lots of 'second skin' dressings and I was on my way. Slowly and very thoughtfully.

That gave me a huge fright, knowing I had just about thrown everything away, but at the same time it helped me focus on the job ahead, the challenge. The next few days were spent frantically trying to fix bike, legs and body.

The stitches only came out the morning I flew out of Blenheim for the first team camp in Auckland. That was where the Paralympic experience really started.

This was the first real team thing I had done, I'd always been very self-contained in terms of both motivation and 'hype'.

The Auckland camp was a chance for everyone to meet, for us to form an identify as the team, 'The New Zealand Team'. It was also a chance for us all to understand the task we had set ourselves. At the first team dinner that evening, Sir Murray Halberg spoke to us. First we watched footage of his gold medal performance at the 1960 Rome Olympics. Even now the intensity of effort and elation brings tears to his eyes. Sir Murray then gave us the most valuable advice ever. What we were about to do he likened to stepping up and opening a new door in our lives. What we needed to do in order to achieve in Sydney was not what we had done to get there, not just our best, but the next level up in every way. He also told us that we would see more free food than ever before in our lives and we must be careful not to eat it. Most thought it very amusing but Sir Murray was very serious. So many careers are sunk in the days leading up to an event in that atmosphere; we had trained to operate in such a specific way at home that any change could be disastrous. And he was so right, we saw so many athletes who sabotaged themselves by overeating and departing from their critical habits.

The Sydney 2000 Paralympic Games, what an event to be at. What a fantastic and awesome environment Sydney provided. To have 3700 elite disabled athletes in one place was both inspiring and humbling for all of us. We (the 'disabled') go through life as pretty unique people in our communities, but there you were just one of many. Everyone there had a story of some sort, everyone had a struggle of some sort, 3700 pretty unique stories in one place. I will always think of it as how the Olympics must have been 30 years or more ago. Very few professionals, everyone had worked hard to get there for the love of their sport, for the challenge.

What a magical experience it turned out to be. I certainly didn't envy Dave Currie (the Chef de Mission) and his team the job of herding the 42 headstrong and frequently lost athletes towards meetings, buses and events. Trying to keep each athlete focused when living in the almost fairytale community of the Olympic Village, with its free everything, 24/7 food and potential 'distractions' around every corner. It couldn't have worked without their professional and committed approach.

We arrived in the village like refugees carting all our belongings with us. We were 'processed' in large warehouse-like buildings — the only thing they didn't have was de-lousing showers. Every vehicle was checked thoroughly for bombs; very serious security for the whole stay, right to the last day.

The New Zealand team was housed in a series of semi-detached town houses on the northern side of the village, about five blocks from the main food hall. Each town house unit had several mobile accommodation units, known as 'portacoms' in its backyard, and I shared one with Paul Jesson for my stay. The first days were all about exploring the village and its diversity. A lot of the athletes knew each other, international paralympic sport isn't a huge club. Training continued in Sydney. I had two events, the road race and the kilo (1000-metre individual time trial), so for two days I needed to peak. My training consisted of fine tuning for the road and technique for the track.

Now the track was always going to be a bit of a wild card for me. While I had trained for it physiologically, I had never actually been on a 250-metre wooden velodrome, ever. After training (and not that often) on an asphalt 440-metre track in breezy Blenheim, to be confronted by an indoor track that looked like the old Fairlie Show 'Wall of Death' was both exciting and scary.

I wasn't so much scared of falling off and doing damage, hell, I had only just finished my antibiotics and still had 'second skin' covering various bits from my last fall. In the elite environment that was the Paralympics, it was the humiliation that I was scared of.

I was, even for my age, the new kid — though you sure forget that you are 41 years old when you first ride the boards (wooden velodrome track), and in an atmosphere like Sydney 2000.

The track is crafted out Norwegian white pine I think, 12° of slope in the short straights and 42° in the corners. Now as a climber I know 42° is steep, you can barely stand up on it, so to get to grips with the idea of cycling around it you need to believe in the laws of physics. My first ride on the velodrome was pretty tentative. Wayne, the cycling manager, really didn't know what he'd been landed with when he saw me circling around the flat getting up the speed and the courage to head up the wall. But up I went and almost yelled with excitement. 'Christ,' I thought, 'I'm really going to nail this.'

For five days the routine was to ride down to the track through the near-lethal Sydney traffic. Every day I realised (and was told) how inexperienced I was, but, rather better, how fast I would be able to go. My 1 minute 29 seconds on the Blenheim track looked like it was going to be a sub 1 minute 25 seconds on the boards, a very respectable time for an old gimp.

As all my training had been at a slower pace, I needed to change the gearing on the track bike but didn't have enough gear with me, so each morning I would be down at the buses at 6 am, bus down to the train and head into the centre of Sydney. I knew of a bike shop that was within three blocks of the train station, so I would be on their doorstep when their doors opened for the day at 8 am. They got to know me in the workshop as I would hunt out a bigger front chain ring or a smaller rear sprocket.

My gear was so basic that Wayne took to calling me the Hillbilly. As a late entrant to bike racing I wasn't steeped in the history and culture of bike racing as most of the other competitors were, this was a wild card event for me after all, not my focus. In fact people tended to use that lack of knowledge to take the piss out of me, some to try and psyche me out, intentionally or otherwise. What most didn't realise is that when you believe in yourself as passionately as I did, then frequently any attempt to psyche you out has the opposite effect. For me it was very much a case of keeping your head down, don't show your hand, then come out and hammer them.

I got pretty damn excited two days out from the kilo when in training I rode a time not too far away from the world record. Wayne had been timing me and even he was getting a bit excited by the whole deal. With his decades of experience, when he started showing confidence in me rather than taking the piss out of me, I knew I was on to a good thing.

The kilo was on day one, the 20th of October 2000, with the opening ceremony on the night of the 19th. With the race the next day, I was considering not going to the opening but compromised by going for the entrance and then sneaking out. While the opening was as spectacular as expected it also turned into a nightmare for me. First we had to queue for hours before the grand entrance — fine if you're sitting in a wheelchair but a bloody pain in the stumps if you have to stand. I'll happily walk for an hour but hate standing still for any more than 15 minutes. I couldn't wear the fashionable team shoes either as they were too heavy and cumbersome, too hard on the stumps. After hours of mucking around, the highlight was definitely the haka — performed twice, once for the Aussies, once in the entrance tunnel for the cameras. It really means something when you are doing it in that environment for your country; it was done with real heart and spirit.

Walking the track with 110,000 people cheering in that stadium is unbeatable. Unfortunately, to leave early meant we had to walk about 4 km, after walking 3 or so to get in. No big deal unless you want to ride the most important race of your life the next day.

The 20th found me nervous and a bit tired. The atmosphere in the velodrome was electric, with music blaring out and the place buzzing. Best of all, Mary and Jim, my mum and dad, were in the gallery, the first race they'd really seen me at, the first race I'd ever really done with an audience. During warm up everyone is checking out everyone else — why I don't know, as the kilo is all about just you, no one else. There are no team tactics, in fact in the kilo there aren't any tactics, just go as hard as humanly possible. Seventeen competitors in the kilo for LC3, and I was 10th off for some reason (just a draw I think). Ten minutes before my time slot as I was taping my legs on, my heart rate was only eight beats above resting. I still can't believe I was that calm.

Then the kilo. From the gun I just focused on going hard. Tony had always told me that if I didn't puke or fall off my bike at the end of the kilo then I hadn't gone fast enough. One minute 23 seconds doesn't sound long, but it is. By the second of the four laps your muscles are starting to burn, by the third they really hurt and the fourth lap is an absolute killer, not just for the pain but actually trying to stay on the steep banked track. Vision blurs, you just desperately want it to finish. I could hear the clack clack clack of the legs working and focused on that sound. I knew I was in a chain ring one tooth too large but you just give it all. Every one of those hard uphill sprints Tony had prescribed was paying dividends.

I didn't puke on Wayne, but he did have to catch me, as when I slowed down I fell off. I was spinning, nauseous and excited as hell. The quickest time so far by almost four seconds, and 30 minutes or so to wait, while the seven fastest LC3 athletes had their own private battle that is the kilo.

Waiting was an exhilarating hell that I wouldn't swap for anything. As I rode in circles cooling down, calming down on my road bike in the centre of the track, each of the last seven gave it their best. Beat, the young Swiss champion, came within 0.1 of a second of my time, far too close to do my heart rate any good, but as each of the others rode I was one place closer to the podium. By the time a bronze was assured I had got off the bike and put my head in my hands. It was all down to fate now, I'd done everything I could (although I was constantly thinking of what I could have done better). As soon as Radovan Kaufman, the world champion, did the first two pedal strokes I knew he would go faster, I didn't even watch, he was storming. Almost two seconds faster, only a breath, but enough to take gold, a fantastic display of power. The sly sod had been telling me only two days earlier that he had been having a terrible year, was ill, had leg problems, felt terrible.

Once it was assured that I had a medal of some sort I had a shadow, a minder. From the second it is confirmed, you have an official at your side who gives you advice about the next stage of the race, because it certainly isn't over until the drug tests are done. I had already had a drink from my own drink bottle, a big 'no no'; only sealed certified drinks should be taken for your own protection (accusing someone of tampering with your drink bottle is not a defence). I was escorted up to the drug testing rooms — locked doors with coded entry, security guards and the 'works', these people sure take what they do very seriously. All the while they were saying, 'Don't worry if you don't want to pee now, we have all day,' while I was saying, 'Please hurry, I really need to pee right now.' I'd had two 'short blacks' before riding, my caffeine kick, and this was playing on my mind. Caffeine is a restricted substance in sport. I'd worked out that I would need six cups to go over the limit, and hadn't had any coffee for weeks so I figured that when I had my two cups I would get a real kick but be well within the limit.

Thirty minutes later standing on the podium, seeing the New Zealand flag go up, I had tears welling up in my eyes. To look up and see Mum and Dad in the gallery and my friends from the Sydney Montana office was all a bit much. It didn't even register that it was 'only a silver', it was as though I'd won the whole world. I was thinking, 'Damn, Anne and the kids should be here,' but we'd planned on them coming over only for my specialist race, the road race.

Standing there, with the bouquet of wild flowers, silver around my neck, was just like standing on Mount Cook or Hicks. The feeling of liberation and motivation was incredible. 'Aoraki/Mount Cook, that's next, time to do it again,' was going through my mind. To have got one of the first medals of the Paralympics was a bit of a bonus as well.

The post-race interviews and photo shoots flew by, and I spent the rest of the day cruising around with a stupid grin all over my face. Calls back home to Anne and the kids, a call to Tony to say thanks as it was his achievement as well. Six long days to wait to the road race, back into the village life and I was starting to feel a bit claustrophobic, time needed to speed up.

Training on the road course started to make me nervous as they had taken the biggest hill out of the course, leaving a 500-metre long, moderately graded hill. Although I would be able to hammer up it, I wouldn't get enough of an advantage to hold on for the following 4 km to the finish line.

Road race day. Anne, Amanda, Jeremy, Mum, Dad, my brother John and his family, plus a host of others turned up to cheer and support. Since the kilo I had gone from nobody to a marked man. Paul and I were both in the same class, same race, so we hoped we'd be able to put something together during the race to bring some more medals home. In reality it became every man for himself, our strengths in riding style actually negating any team advantage, I think. While I was able to lead the field up the hill, stretching all but two of them to the max, Paul would almost by default pull the whole field back to us down the other side as he caught up and powered past us.

It was the dirtiest race I have ever been in; two riders went down, and I ended up riding right over one poor sod. Tony and I had planned that I should stay up near the front, let others do the work, and not do any silly breaks unless I could work with someone. The pace was actually quite slow, 35–40 kmh only, and Paul was continually yelling to up the pace (go faster to hurt the weaker riders and split the field), breaking off the front regularly only to be pulled back by the nine Europeans all acting as a team. There really was little chance of us two and the one Aussie, Noel, working against a 'team' of nine. There was jersey pulling, spitting in your face, clipping your wheels and shouldering — bugger that.

For the last half of the race I put on a few breaks off the front, otherwise sat near the back out of the way. On the last lap I was near the lead over the hill but got swamped shortly afterwards, two corners from the finish, and they biffed me into the crash barrier. I only just stayed upright (and still have the grazes on my carbon legs). The final sprint was set up to negate my sprint as the 'European train' wound it from 2 km out, going into the sprint at 50 kmh, too high for me to bridge the gap that had developed and too fast for me to sustain. We nearly all finished on the same time as one big bunch, the wheel I was behind (Kaufman's) was fourth, I was a disappointing 12th. 'Thank God for the kilo,' was going through my mind repeatedly as I went over the finish line: time to have a wine, something decent and fattening to eat and start thinking about going home. And that was exactly what we did that night: a family dinner at an exciting Italian restaurant on Oxford Street, a few wines and time to wind down.

What an event though, the commitment by everyone from day one showed through with the medal haul. The final parties were in full swing around Sydney, and we were hosted at a variety of venues and Montana were very generous in donating wine for the team's final party. I know it sounds like sacrilege, but the spectacular closing ceremony and party were a bit of a bore for me: 'Come on, I've got some really important projects I want to get on with at home!'

On the flight home, the gold medallists all got upgraded to business class. The comment in economy class down the back was that if we had only known, we might have been able to try that bit harder — anything to get out of cattle class.

Back home in New Zealand, the strength of the goodwill humbled us all. For me it was really apparent back in Blenheim. The first outing was the annual Marlborough Mistletoe Market, a pre-Christmas market on the streets of central Blenheim. It took Anne and me all morning to get from one end to the other, about three blocks.

The weeks after my return were hectic. I was still buzzing, not just with my silver, but because the potential I had shown over there meant that at the coming New Zealand Track Championships I would have a chance at the world record for the kilo. I knew that if I'd been smarter it would have been mine in Australia, and I was determined it would be mine in February at the velodrome in Dunedin.

It wasn't to be. Those weeks of hectic work, travel and catching up at home with family and chores meant spending many hours on my walking legs. After spending hours per day on the bike in the previous three or four months, in my highly modified carbon bike legs, and being careful to recover from training fully (not overexerting myself by walking too much) I wasn't used to the standard walking legs. The continual hammering caused a type of DVT (deep vein thrombosis) to flare up in the back of my left stump, making any weight-bearing on that leg almost impossible. Walking was agony, riding just not an option, so the idea of breaking any record evaporated.

Once again I became a regular at the hospital, getting ultrasound studies done and visiting the specialist. The option of surgery on a weight-bearing part of my stump wasn't at all attractive: two or three months off my stump would destroy a year of build up, and put me on crutches when I hate being disabled. To control the pain the specialist put me on some anti-inflammatories and the effect was miraculous: pain gone immediately and within days I was back on the bike and my legs. But those two weeks had taken the edge off my form, meaning back to square one.

One of the perks to arise out of Sydney was an invite to Paul Holmes's Christmas party, based around the 'Cirque de Soleil' extravaganza. All the medallists were there, a great chance to catch up after the event and get a preview of the exciting gymnastic circus. Holmes had been a great supporter of the Paralympics, involved with the televising of the event since Barcelona in 1992 I think. Not just the athletes but many of the television production team were there too.

With a climb of Cook fizzing away in my brain, I spied Chas Toogood. Chas and his team had done the live broadcast from Sydney for TV and had a background in TV production that only someone with a surname like Toogood could have. We were waiting for a taxi before we all turned into pumpkins at midnight, and it seemed as good a time as any to corner him.

'Hi Chas, want to do a doco on a climb of Mount Cook by a legless winemaker with steel and titanium legs?'

The response was an instant yes, and a swapping of contact numbers so we could confirm that the chat wasn't just one of those midnight rash statements.

Chas first asked, 'Why? Why climb Cook again?'

'Easy,' I said. 'It's a great idea, an adventure. But more seriously it's just time. It's taken 15 years of feeling nostalgic and sorry for myself every November 29th, 15 years of sitting at home watching tapes of the various footage filmed about the event. Anne used to pretend she had forgotten the significance of the date, as I was never the happiest of people at the time. But now I celebrate the event, and what better way than to stand on the top again, show people ability, show myself ability.'

Why a documentary? Easy, I knew that with it would come a lot of the resources I needed to do the climb, to get sponsorship for gear which would cost thousands, thousands we as a family didn't have. The only problem with it was that as soon as it was said, as soon as the intention was voiced, for me there was no going back. As I was to find out over the coming months, it was a bit like having a tiger by the tail.

8 BEEN AWAY TOO LONG: MOUNT COOK 2001

AFTER OPENING MY GOB to Chas, what seemed to be just a good idea quickly turned into a tangible project, planned for December 2001.

Job number one was to get a project to develop suitable climbing legs funded and up to speed. Wayne and I had a conference presentation for Carter Holt Harvey's Kinleith mill staff, done in Te Papa under the Britten V1000. It was a fantastic chance to link the bike's innovation with the development of the cycling leg. Interestingly, one of the audience, Steve Kast, was a climber we had rescued back in 1982 (I think), helicoptering him off the De le Beche ridge with a broken ankle. This connection generated a sponsorship agreement that provided Wayne with some funds to develop the 'Alped' legs. The original idea was that Steve would come down to Mount Cook to support me on the mountain, but as the year went on I became increasingly nervous about the number of people who would be on the mountain for whom I would feel (indirectly) responsible. So that part of the scheme was dropped, unfortunately for Steve who had done a lot of training, but the numbers were getting too high.

The funding was the bare minimum for Wayne. He had a vision for the Alpeds: to make the ultimate all-terrain leg, to maximise traction and feel on all surfaces. I should have known not to be surprised, but the first sight of what looked like Arnie's feet from *Terminator* was still a buzz — where does he come up with the ideas? The concept looked great, and the first walk had me striding across the yard looking for a slope to test them on straight away. They were far from perfect, very dynamic in action, but lacking finesse, great potential if they got a bit of polishing.

I had a trip to Europe planned and due to start in September, which was closing fast, and with Wayne due to be away in North America when I got back, there wasn't going to be much time for development of the Alpeds. In fact we lost all of September and October — not that there was much time in July or August either.

The Europe trip was for three reasons: first to race at the 2001 European Disabled Cycling Championships in Switzerland; followed by two weeks in France looking at winemaking in Champagne, Burgundy and Alsace; and, lastly, almost four weeks in England and Scotland presenting wines in the trade for Montana. Anne was to join me after Switzerland for three weeks of travel, the first time we had travelled together overseas. So two months of my training for Mount Cook was going to be done in Europe; not ideal but there just isn't enough time in life really.

Before Europe, as always, vintage intervened. Once again I was attempting to maintain some training during those intense weeks. I did less than other years, which was a bit better for my health but not so hot for my riding. Just to complicate matters further, Anne and I finally decided to go ahead with some house renovations, not to the extent that we wanted as we couldn't afford it, but still a significant amount of work to be done and a lot of large cheques to write. As September got closer, the work and training all concertina'd up, with the only bright spot being an overnight respite at the Wharekauhau Resort in the Wairarapa, compliments of a firm who wanted me to do a presentation on the evening of our wedding anniversary.

Needless to say I stepped on a plane for Zurich on the 1st of September leaving Anne with the last stages of the renovations to supervise and pay for — I don't think I would get away with that again though.

If it wasn't for the cost involved, and the money already paid, then I wouldn't have gone to the European Champs. Ten days before going I was struck down with the flu, the only year recently that I haven't had a flu jab. I hadn't been that sick in years: five days in bed feeling like death, and as weak as a kitten and coughing my lungs up for another few days. While I recovered my strength quickly, I had no endurance left.

I wasn't to be by myself in Zurich. Paul Ward, a wingy (arm amputee) from Auckland, was there for his first international experience and Chas Toogood had arranged to be in Switzerland with cameras ready in time for the racing. Luckily I had allowed five days in Zurich to get over jet lag and recover from the flu with a minimum of pressure, but the busy year had taken its toll.

I pulled out of the pursuit and only raced (somewhat feebly) the kilo. The track was an outdoor concrete 333-metre oval, with very long straights and very steep (52° I think) tight corners. A bumpy, technical track. Quite a challenge for Paul first time out but a good learning experience; any other track will be easy for him after that one. All the competitors from Sydney were there and a few new faces as well. Unfortunately, unlike Sydney, I was no longer an unknown quantity and got the top seeding, meaning I would race last. Everyone before me was riding about three seconds slower than their Sydney times, which would put me at about 1 minute 26 seconds for the 1000 metres. After training I thought I might squeeze out 1 minute 27 seconds if I could hang on in that last lap, but I couldn't: 1 minute 29 seconds, almost as slow as the old track in Blenheim and only good enough for eighth, beaten even by Noel, my regular Australian competitor. And of course it was all on film, thanks to Chas.

The day after the kilo, four days before we were to ride the road race, that terrible event that changed how we view the world was played out on CNN: September 11.

Following a training ride in the early afternoon, I got out of the shower, flicked the TV on and saw one of the World Trade Center towers burning. I just thought it was a disaster movie until the second plane dived in right before my eyes. It still took some minutes for my mind to comprehend the enormity of the tragedy. After watching for a while, my concern was for the American team, racing the pursuit down at the track. The Kiwis had built up many close friendships with the riders and staff of the US team; they were always ready to lend the poor Kiwis a hand at events, as it was rare for us to have any support. Additionally, their mechanic was a Kiwi, Mark Legg, a highly rated cyclocross rider studying in the US. I hopped on the team vehicle (my bike) and headed down to the track. I took the manager and the coach aside and broke the news to them: the last thing the athletes needed was that sort of news dumped on them right before an important race. By the time I returned to the hotel we had armed soldiers on every floor for security.

The Champs went on, though everyone was in shock. For me the road race followed, well three-quarters of the road race, as while I was keeping with the bunch they were just cruising, and every attack or break left me coughing my lungs up. Time to pack up and head for the UK to pick up Anne. For both of us, flying in the week post September 11 was somewhat nerve-racking, me with all of my gear getting thoroughly searched, and Anne having the joy of flying within sight of Afghanistan.

The rest of the trip was a whirlwind of travel and presentations. I had my bike in London but was too chicken to take on the traffic most days. Training for Aoraki/Mount Cook was limited to every morning in the gym on the stair climber or a spin bike.

New Zealand in November wasn't much quieter than it had been before I left, but at least I was able to get out hill running and biking regularly, using my flex feet as Wayne hadn't yet got back from America to finish the Alpeds. The tall tanks and catwalks in the winery came in very handy for practising crevasse rescue and abseiling techniques.

With the climb getting nearer and more real by the day, December was hectic: finalising gear for the climb; worrying about financing; worrying about blending and stabilising the wines at Montana; and trying to train for both cycling and the climb. The wet summer didn't help, in fact it made things worse as it reminded me of 1982.

The disturbed weather patterns, with the highs (anticyclones) too far north so they skipped across the top of New Zealand, mirrored the patterns of the 1982–83 summer, El Niño all over again. Instead of the relatively calm and settled summers of the last six years, continual westerlies were bringing wild weather to the Southern Alps. After the severe Marlborough droughts of the last few years, it seemed most unfair that the pattern had to pick that year to break.

Wayne had sent up the final version of the Alpeds, the climbing legs, just in time for the last three weeks of training. I started using them intensively on the hill behind the winery, walking and running up the hill, a 120-metre high coastal bump with a steep four-wheel-drive track up it. When running (well, staggering fast) up that hill the legs felt fantastic, I could get some real power down on the ground. The hand-shaped forefoot would mould over any irregularities, requiring far less concentration and care in foot placement. Unfortunately I got so carried away with my new-found ability that I was still breaking them a bit too easily. That dreaded metallic ping and snap noise, the sound of spring steel breaking, was a sound I didn't want to hear on Mount Cook, that's for sure. The thought that it might happen half way up the summit rocks or on the hard ice of the ice cap wasn't pleasant.

But these were prototype legs, so testing the boundaries involved hearing that noise more than once. The first time it happened was weeks earlier, while trialling the legs up high on the ridge to Mount Hutt ski field. The terrain there is subalpine scrub and tussock with rocky outcrops linked by scree slopes. The legs were working fantastically well on this alpine scrambling type of terrain. They were so active in their action that they seemed to almost levitate me up the hill, with the spring off the toe almost throwing my feet up. Even going up the unstable scree slopes, which is difficult enough with flesh-and-blood models, they had a fantastic traction, that hand-like forefoot moulding itself to the ground like a large suction pad. The heel, with its soft action and narrow profile, gave great stability and cushioning coming downhill, always the hardest on the stumps.

I wasn't on them long before I was looking for rock outcrops to practise climbing on, and scree slopes to run down. I still had misgivings about several elements of their action though, mostly to do with what they would be like in more difficult technical rock-climbing conditions. I had been spoilt in the past with my stiff, light, carbon fibre legs in the ultra-sticky rubber of rock boots. That combination had always performed brilliantly on even the smallest footholds, but the Alpeds were looking to be inferior in that respect.

Mount Hutt was the first time since we had started the leg project that I got a real insight into how much potential these *Terminator* look-alike legs really had. It was also the first time I had enough confidence in the design to commit to them; confidence that they would get me up Aoraki/Mount Cook. Up until that point we had only used the prototypes on tarseal, a very different proposition from the mountains. I was still nervous about their performance on technical rock, but for the climb planned I was hoping to be able to leave my crampons on for the whole climb, even the summit rocks.

In my enthusiasm I started running up the ski-field road, revelling in the feedback generated by the spring action, almost bounding up the track, yelling and whooping, until that dreaded 'ping'. I almost collapsed onto my left knee, the left foot was as soft as marshmallow and had gone all floppy. The feeling when it breaks is an instantaneous transition from the leg being a dynamic, active body part to standing on a really narrow peg (try stilts some time). I guess I demonstrated my attitude to leg design to Wayne when I then started bouncing up and down on the right one, getting great 'air' until it gave way as well, snapping the spring in a similar place. Better that I test it to destruction on Mount Hutt than on Aoraki/Mount Cook.

For Wayne it wasn't so much back to the drawing board as back to analyse the break, refine the spring technology and make it beefier. 'If it doesn't break during design then it's over engineered', was one of Wayne's catch-cries.

The new version arrived at work in the mail, with a note telling me to wear the springs in slowly, give them a few hours' work before getting carried away. I tried, but the temptation to use them to the max was too great — yep, back to running up that hill.

By the time I headed south, we were on 8-mm diameter springs in the feet, up from the original 6-mm springs we had started with. I knew that I could make them do the job, but only with some care — not the most comfortable position to be in, but in many respects running up a tussock-covered hill was always going to be a harder test than plodding up the Linda Glacier. Bullet-proof legs would have been great, but with no more development time or money available, it would have meant legs that were just too heavy. Life's always a bit of a compromise. Unfortunately, in the mountains there isn't a lot of leeway for learning, so we had to be very careful that it was the right compromise.

With the final version of the legs broken again on that hill behind the winery, and the climb upon us, I left the legs in Wayne's hands as I passed through Christchurch. The plan was for him to rebuild them overnight and be in Mount Cook in 36 hours' time with them ready for the climb.

I felt nervous leaving Christchurch without the legs, though I knew they needed to be rebuilt. It was a bit like travelling without your wallet. You might get away with it for a while but you'll need it sooner or later and you won't want to wait until it is delivered.

The weather had been so terrible in the Southern Alps in spring and early summer that if I had arrived at Mount Cook and everything had looked perfect, then I think I would have started without the legs. I would have been sitting at Plateau Hut waiting for them to be flown in, or if the weather had been brilliant I might have even climbed without them. No one knows better than me just how precious fine weather and good conditions are in the mountains of the Southern Alps.

Driving south from Christchurch it really started to feel like an adventure. Partly it was escape from the pressures of the last months and partly the realisation that this adventure had a feeling of correctness to it, the place where I really should be. My new little Vitara (if you can call a six-year-old car new) felt so natural and having Amanda, now 12 and only a year away from high school, for company was great fun for both of us. Anne and Lucy were travelling down the next day, as we never seem to have enough room for everyone and everything in one car, mostly due to having too many toys on board, like road bikes, mountain bikes, climbing gear and all the accompanying bits and pieces. Jeremy had decided to stay at home to work in the Montana vineyards — he was lusting after a new road racing bike so had lots of hours to do to raise the funds.

While I was pleased to have the family along, I was also quite nervous, as before a climb I generally like to be by myself or at least to not have to deal with others. I expect everyone to be self-sufficient and of use, which is difficult if you are new to a sport or culture and don't know what is expected. Selfish I know, but very important for the 'head' preparation, for going into a challenge like a climb (or a race) with everything on your side. In hindsight, from what I've learnt about handling some of these challenges over the years, that attitude was possibly an indication that I wasn't prepared enough; I was still too stressed to see clearly.

We stopped for the night in Geraldine with Mum and Dad. The idea of me going climbing again, especially on Aoraki/Mount Cook, wasn't that easy on Mum, or on any of the rest of the family. A huge adventure for me though, and a great opportunity to show the kids another part of my past. Mum was very keen on my having a quick successful climb and 'getting it over with'. One comment was: 'Once you've done the climb what are you going to do with all that gear?' I didn't have the heart to say 'find something bigger' though Amanda, the ratbag, made sure she knew that was the idea.

Driving from Geraldine to Mount Cook has always been a magical journey for me. So many years of travelling to and from Mount Cook has instilled in me a love of driving, of travelling, even over these same roads time and time again. What a pity they don't have the lookout at

Pukaki anymore — the old one as you came across the lake's terminal moraine on your way from Tekapo. It had always been a hugely nostalgic place for me, as from there I could see all those routes I'd done over the years on Mount Cook and its surrounding mountains, and I used to marvel at how I'd ever done some of them.

Sunday lunch was spent catching up with Charlie, who I had met in the late seventies climbing in South Canterbury, now a mountain ski guide with his own company Southern Alps Guiding, and Mary in their Twizel sanctuary: a great escape, like going back 20 years, catching up on families and friends, both those still around and those gone on. The afternoon was spent planning the next week, as Charlie, as well as being my rope mate and guide, was organising all the ancillary equipment and staff (guides, safety staff for the film crew and helicopters), looking at the weather maps, a bit of gear checking and yet another brew of tea, all creating an atmosphere as though I had never left. This was a part of my life I had missed, tied up in the intense world of corporate winemaking. For me mountaineering was all about the culture as much as the physical side of it, so it was great to be immersed in it again.

No time to dawdle though, it was the 65 km up to the Hermitage to get my first taste of the media circus that was to come. A BBC film crew was waiting for me. They were filming for the *The Ray Mear's Extreme Survival Show*, a BBC2 documentary based around survival stories, including re-creations, with the aim of providing lessons for anyone in similar situations.

I wandered up to the first swing bridge with Ray, the host, Martin, the producer, and the crew. We found a boulder to sit on in among the jumbled terminal moraine of the Mueller glacier. These moraines have huge table- or house-like boulders scattered around, with regenerating alpine scrub, and mountains providing a dramatic backdrop. It was as much a chat as an interview; sitting there you can see right down the valley to the Hermitage and Mount Cook village. You could almost see the Park Headquarters and the heli-pad. All the old memories of flying in and out of the heli-pad, the great and dramatic times in my life, came flooding back. It was one of the most emotional interviews I had ever done — that is, until a few days later. The film crew didn't quite realise how close I was to tears at times, tears both of joy at just being back with a mission, and of nostalgia (I told them shortly after they shouted me dinner though).

In one of those great coincidences in life they asked who I derived inspiration from. When I said Norman Croucher (the UK double amputee climber) they all looked up including the camera man. 'I was at Norman's birthday party last week, he lives just down the road,' he said, while the camera carried on filming my left ear and nothing much else.

The next day, Monday, dawned fine but with a rising nor-wester. I put in a morning call to Charlie to discuss the weather, which had the look of 'great now but turning to crap soon' as it so often does. I found that even though I hadn't lived in the mountains since 1985 I was still completely in tune with the weather and its patterns. I guess I had learnt so much, especially in the last years at the park giving climbing advice, that it was really still second nature to me.

Walking out of the front doors of the Hermitage, Antony from TV3 came up to say hi. I was thinking, 'What are you up here for? Something big must be going on,' so it was quite a surprise to find out it was me, but this turned out to be only the thin edge of the wedge for the week to come. He asked for some time to do an interview, so I winked at Charlie and suggested that any interview would look best at a place like the Grand Plateau. It meant 40 minutes or so of helicopter time so I took a step back when he said that would be great. We did a deal to talk in the afternoon and if we had decided that we weren't going into the hills because of the threatening weather then they would fly us somewhere else for the interview (I love hello's, if you hadn't guessed).

The early part of the day was spent doing the team circus thing (with film crew, their guides and Wayne, who had now arrived up from his Christchurch Britten workshop with my Alpeds), meeting people and setting the rules for survival in the hills. It was interesting to see the attitudes of some of the crew who were inexperienced in our high alpine conditions. You have to see and experience the real mountains in New

Zealand to understand what you have let yourself in for; it took a bit of beating into some at first.

Every hour for the rest of that first day there was a check of the weather, and bit by bit Charlie and I could see the situation deteriorating. There were climbers flying into the Grand Plateau by the bucketful and the thought of spending three days in a big Plateau storm with 30 smelly climbers didn't seem that attractive really. Must be getting old.

Later in the afternoon, with a bit of negotiation, Charlie and I flew to Plateau with the TV3 film crew. It was a great flight, we even managed to talk Brendon the pilot into a brief excursion up the mouth of the Linda Glacier canyon to look at the route we were planning on climbing. It actually looked good for the time of the year, reasonably navigable, not too broken by the huge crevasses it is renowned for. From the Squirrel helicopter we could even see a route up the lower third of the glacier, usually the most broken. Landing near Plateau Hut in worsening weather, I felt like a bit of a prat poncing (also called stumbling) around for the camera and doing an interview while all the Plateau Hut climbers were looking on. The snow conditions didn't inspire confidence, about 200 mm of fresh wet snow with a slight crust. We only had an ice axe so we didn't wander too far from the hut area, just up the slope towards Glacier Dome to get away from the helicopter noise. The weather was marginal enough that the pilot kept the helicopter's blades turning ready for a quick exit; no turning the engine off this time.

After flying out I couldn't believe it when Brendon said as we landed that there was another crew waiting to do the same thing. First inclination was to say no as I thought that without my Lekis (walking poles like adjustable ski poles) I was stumbling around like a drunk. Then I settled on yes but let's go somewhere different please, like Darwin Corner up on the Tasman Glacier. So there I was, doing the same again, although I was pleased to find each reporter had their own style and angle to reduce the monotony. Great to get into another part of the mountains — thanks TV1 — was my mercenary view.

The first thing I did when I got down though was to get Wayne to cut 20 mm off the leg pylons. When moving on the slippery soft snow I could instantly feel a continual leverage on the stumps that compromised control and would quickly cause stump damage.

While all this was buzzing about me, Anne, Lucy and Amanda were on the periphery, dealing with a combination of being bored, fascinated and left out. Climbing is a bit like cycle racing in heaps of ways, especially where the family or spectators are concerned. There are lots of technical terms which we expect everyone to know and lots of cold shouldering of people not in the 'team'. All very evident now but less so then.

It was obvious we wouldn't get in that day. The team met several times to look at the latest weather maps on the Internet and match them up to what was happening outside. There would be no climbing for two days, but there was a promising-looking weather pattern developing for later in the week. What followed was two days of luxury hanging around the Hermitage feeling like a total fraud. Even in our days living in the village, Anne and I had never had the experience of the luxury hotel. Dennis and Christine Callesen were superb hosts for those two days, hosting barbecues for the family and introducing us all to new friends. We took the opportunity to have a 'team' dinner, an elegant feast crafted by the Hermitage chefs, and matched with some of the best wines from around the world. It was an opportunity for me to say thanks to everyone for getting us so far and for what I hoped we would achieve over the next few days. It also gave me a chance to do the winemaker thing, describing the wines and the stories behind them, something I love to do.

The weather at Cook was as terrible as we had expected, a strong nor-west flow bringing gale force winds, cloud and snow to the mountains, and the wind stronger, if anything, down in the valleys. To make the best of the time we headed down the valley to practise some rope work on the Pukaki Boulder (near the end of Lake Pukaki), a favourite haunt of climbers on bad weather days. The boulder is a huge rock on the old lateral moraine, deposited there by the glacier tens of thousands of years ago. Even down there we had to be careful in the wind; it was tricky just standing up on the four–metre rock in the gusting wind. It was a great chance for Charlie to check out my memory for rope handling and glacier travel.

In climbing, the rope is a critical life-line, frequently misunderstood by those who have never had the opportunity to climb. My rope is a 60–metre nylon umbilical cord, only 9.5–mm thick but capable of holding well over a ton of force. The rope actually has the ability to stretch under load, both softening the effects of a fall and also softening the load on your anchors. It's not much use being roped up when climbing unless one person is attached to the mountain in some way. The two notable exceptions are in guiding situations and in glacier travel.

When travelling on glaciers the main danger comes from what you can't see: hidden crevasses. Glaciers, with their continual river-like movement, crack and split in places, a bit like river rapids, and form crevasses. They are frequently covered with snow, so you never quite know where they are, or, if you do, then you won't know how strong the snow bridge is. With two climbers roped together, usually about 15 metres apart, if one drops into a 'slot' the other needs to hold their weight, place an anchor such as an ice axe or snow stake in the snow and tie the other climber off to it. Once this is done the unlucky victim in the crevasse can either use 'prussiks' (short loops of cord tied to the rope with 'slip' knots) to climb up the rope or get pulled up. The consequences of a fall into a crevasse mirror those of a car accident — it's not the fall that kills or maims, it's the stopping at the bottom. With guiding, the superior skill and technique of the guide means he or she can move together with a client on a short rope, controlling any small slip or fall almost instantly on quite steep and exposed pitches. Once the likelihood or consequences of a fall become more serious then even guides revert to pitch climbing with one of the party tied to the mountain at all times, the other moving with confidence knowing that if they fall, they won't go further than the length of the rope.

The rope technology hadn't really changed much in the last 20 years, my new rope replacing the one left on Middle Peak being slightly lighter and just as expensive. The good thing about playing around down at the Pukaki Boulder was that I rapidly became more confident in my ability to hold Charlie if he dropped into a slot.

Crevasse rescue practice, Pukaki Boulder, December 2001.

The cloud on the horizon though was that the damn legs performed terribly on the small edge holds, meaning I managed to make a real fool of myself in front the film crews. Even mucking around on a boulder the size of a truck was enough to attract the cameras. It was a good chance for Chas and the film crew to try wiring us up for sound on the mountain and for the team to familiarise themselves with the gear.

I hung around the rock for a few hours, practising abseiling, lowering, setting up my prussik loops and organising my harness and the gear that hangs off it. For the trip up the Linda Glacier the rope would be set up for glacier travel, with about 15 loops of excess rope around my shoulders, and the rope end and the last loop attached to the harness. On the rope in front of me I had a prussik loop already attached to the rope as well, with other loops hanging off a karabiner (a metal clip that climbers use to connect themselves to ropes and other gear) on my harness, ready for use if the worst happened. A short sling was also

The team trialling rope and film work, Pukaki Boulder.

Above: The team at the Hermitage, December 2001; Lucy, Amanda and Anne are in the foreground.

Below: On the balcony at the Hermitage in typical nor'wester conditions; cloud coming over the main divide and hogsbacks on Mount Cook.

Above: The top of the Linda Glacier route: Linda Shelf and couloirs on the left, summit rocks rising on the left skyline with the ice cap reaching up to the summit in the distance.

Mary Hobbs/*New Zealand Outside*

Left: Absolutely gutted and trying to show a brave face: Charlie (right) and I on the Grand Plateau after the December attempt.

Above: Wearing my 'Alped' feet on the Tasman Glacier, December 2001.

Above: After over 20 years, back on Aoraki: better than being on the podium at Sydney.

Below: It's a long way down: Charlie (right) and I moving onto the summit of Aoraki.

ary Hobbs/*New Zealand Outside*

Above: Being filmed by Mark Whetu on the hard ice below the summit rocks.

Above: Soft snow over hard ice, the final slog up the summit ice cap; the Grand Plateau is far below.

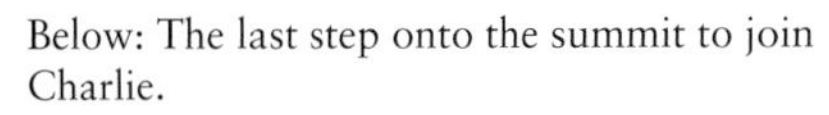

Below: The last step onto the summit to join Charlie.

attached, with a locking karabiner to tie onto anchors where necessary.

All ready to go, now we only needed the weather to play the game.

There is nothing worse than hanging around waiting for the weather. I've never been known for patience. To fill in the time, apart from the regular checking of the weather maps, I headed out on the mountain bike. The rules had changed a lot since I last lived in the village, so the riding was limited to the few gravel roads in the area, but exploring up the Tasman Valley was fun, revisiting some of the secluded beautiful spots I was privileged enough to know.

The clouds disappeared on Wednesday evening, too late to fly in which was frustrating; the summit of Aoraki/Mount Cook looked so tempting and so close in the evening light. But Thursday would be the day.

After a monster breakfast on Thursday morning the team converged on the airport to sort gear and await the helicopter ride to the Grand Plateau. The team consisted of Charlie (friend, guide and chief organiser), Mark Whetu (mountain camera), Dave McKinlay ('Narly', safety for Whetu), Wayne as mechanic, Mark Woodward ('Woody', guide for Wayne), Dave McLeod ('Spoon', hut guide and organiser, looking after the camera crew), Chas Toogood (producer and director of our doco, *No Mean Feat*), Hamish Wilson (camera), Don Anderson (sound) and me of course. Still to arrive was Peter Thompson with his helicopter-mounted camera to film the climbing from the air. With all the camera gear, personal gear, bodies, and enough food to ruin any diet, it turned into two flights for the Squirrel up to Plateau.

And what a circus Plateau turned out to be. We couldn't simply land of course, we had to do it several times for the cameras; no one complained too much though, as it looked spectacular. The whole circus was a bit of an omen really, as I hate being the centre of that level of attention, and I was starting to feel uncomfortable. Not so much that I am 'camera shy' as 'people shy'. I am always very conscious of having earned the right to do things, I was worried about causing disruption before climbing Cook again; after would have been fine, I'd have had the credentials to do anything.

There were so many climbers in Plateau Hut that the thought of being crammed in there with the camera crew and constantly having to interact with the other climbers was too much for me. Also, the climbers had just been through four days or so of storm conditions, virtually trapped in the close confines of the hut, so the last thing I wanted to do was make them more cramped with a film crew and our party. When I saw Dave McKinlay ('Narly') putting up his tent on a small snow ledge 10 metres from the hut I immediately asked if there was room for two. Luckily the answer was yes and we all then had a magical afternoon and evening in one of the most spectacular places on earth, in perfect clear weather. The afternoon was burningly hot, the combination of a perfect day, the altitude and snow reflection making even SPF 30 sun block seem wimpy.

Charlie and I took the opportunity of the great day to head up the slopes of Glacier Dome behind Plateau Hut. We worked on our glacier travel and roping techniques, already like second nature to me again. More importantly we trialled the snowshoes that Charlie brought as a backup for soft conditions. They were a revelation, keeping me up on the snow, and providing a really stable platform. Because of the split foot platform of the legs, without the snowshoes I did a real gimpy sideways slipping thing, especially on sun-softened afternoon snow. The design of the Alpeds also meant that my 66 kg weight was pressing through a smaller area than 'real' legs so in fact my body was acting like it was at least 100 kg. The snowshoes corrected that problem, though it did take a bit of practice to master the sweeping shuffling gait necessary to move comfortably and fast with them on.

The rest of the afternoon was spent lying in the tent trying to rest up. But every minute in there was another minute listening to the wind rise. We had one of Narly's famous dinners (always pick guides or climbing partners who are chefs) at about 7 pm then back to the tent. As always, I tried to sort out my gear into what to carry (too much), what to wear, what to leave behind. Then try to sleep — yeah right, the combination of excitement, nerves and the thought of 'here goes' meant a cat nap at best.

Alarm goes at 11 pm though no need really. I can see the lights of the film crew, hear Charlie up and about, worrying about the wind and keen to get way. Repack everything done four hours earlier, think harder about it and repack again. Breakfast, always hard at midnight, but manage to stuff down some bread and Weet-Bix. More cameras, more people, and feeling a bit stressed and nervous. Stumps have that tender feeling that gives me a bad feeling. Even being up so early we still get away late (12.30 am) as Charlie is reminding me, so I remind him I was happy to go three hours ago. I really don't think the guys have understood my requirements, my limitations, but what the hell, we're here now.

At Plateau you need to rope up from right outside the hut as the first slope leads into a crevasse field. From the first few steps I knew things weren't going to be easy. The freeze we were relying on had only partially occurred. The snow wasn't hard enough for me to stay on the surface. Even the footprints formed the day before hadn't frozen enough for my climbing legs; they were continually punching through even deeper. In the dark (actually the light of our head lamps) this causes two problems: extra energy and effort are involved in plugging 'new' steps; and, worse, being continually slightly off-balance causes tearing and rubbing of the sockets.

So in that strange half light we descended a few hundred metres in the tracks and then put the snowshoes on. The plateau is a huge ice field lying under the eastern flanks of Mount Cook, Tasman, Dixon and the other main divide peaks. It is about 1.5 km from Plateau Hut across to the mouth of the canyon the Linda Glacier has formed.

I had forgotten how far we had to descend straight after leaving the hut; two big partially frozen snow slopes. The snow that morning was perfect for those who had legs but with every step, with or without the snowshoes, I struck a difficulty of some sort. I really wished I had someone in front to make small, really firm steps so that the two-piece *Terminator* legs could sit nicely in them rather than being the very unstable platforms they were proving to be in those conditions. Someone to take the pack weight would have been great too.

Once we were almost across the Plateau and into the mouth of the

Linda Glacier we struck the first frustration — wrong route. We followed the wrong set of steps and ended up in a crevasse field unable to go forward, 'bluffed' as trampers would say. I must admit thinking and yelling out loud to Woody and Wayne up in front, 'What sort of bloody guides are you?' That wee excursion was only 10 or 15 minutes out of the way at the most, but in my nervous state it seemed like half the mountain. I knew I had only a fixed amount of time on my legs, so every small incident that 'wasted' that time was as painful to me as pulling teeth.

Even at this early stage (an hour of glacier travel from the hut) I was getting a bit frustrated at not getting rid of more weight to Wayne or someone. Charlie and I could see their lights 200 metres up the mountain above us — 'No use you being up there if the legs break, mate,' was all I could think.

The Linda at night: you only see flashes of what's around you in the light from your head lamps, but you know there's the equivalent of a horror movie playing above your heads in the ice cliffs in the dark. Amazing sight in the morning when you look down at what you have just ascended — and what you now need to climb down!

As the morning wore on we wound our way up through the maze of crevasses. After about two hours I had to take the snowshoes off and rely on the steps already formed in the semi-frozen snow, as the slopes go too steep and hard. Up until then they had been a real life-saver, giving me a broad, stable platform and the freedom to step where I liked. The most difficult bits were those that I had predicted — teetering along arêtes (knife-sharp narrow ridges) with huge slots either side. It was damn lucky it was dark and we couldn't see into their depths. The few steep steps were a bit of a challenge with only one axe and a leki pole, but I didn't have an easy system to swap the poles for ice tools. It's one of those things that seems simple on a warm day at sea level, but in the dark, when you are ice cold and wearing all the paraphernalia associated with glacier travel it's an energy-sapping pain. We only stopped momentarily through the lower Linda as it is just so dangerous. I guess if you don't know the climb you can just cruise, but all of us except

Wayne were cursed with knowing every ice cliff hanging over us and every accident that has claimed a life in this area.

Eventually we stopped, once we were past Teichelmann's Corner and the main avalanche danger area, to eat, or at least try to (my PowerBars were frozen solid and so was I soon after). Charlie put some clothes on. I didn't drink as it was too much hassle and effort to get my bag off and dick around — which actually showed that the effects of not having eaten enough food were kicking in. Quite amazing really, as on the bike I would never let my body get into that state. I religiously drink and eat at the right times, priding myself on my 'feel' and understanding of my body and, as a consequence, I am able to ride for hours on end. This time I didn't really have my act together so I didn't get the fuel.

I was sure that the Bowie Ridge bivvy site was near and we would have a good rest, plenty of food and perhaps a hot drink. So a long trudge up for another hour, but it seemed like several as I was still punching in through a crust every few steps, getting more and more tired, and wrecking the stumps. Bowie corner when it finally arrived was really cold and windy. Then the bloody helicopter came in to film and blew me about, which didn't help. I found it difficult to get clothes on and off, let alone lever and wire the crampons onto the legs. It seemed like I had to take more clothes off to get more on and by then I was really cold — not enough fuel in the tank for sure.

I hadn't been that cold in years, my brain just wasn't in the right space. The cold and tiredness started to bring on hand and stump cramps. A few shots of Cramp Stop helped, but I knew then that it was probably over. I didn't tell anyone of course. I thought there was still a chance that once I had rested and warmed up the growing pain and cramps would go away. After all, you can see the summit from there. I knew that the next few hours would be extremely difficult as the prospect of failure had already crept into my mind.

From the Bowie the slopes steepen into a chute that avalanches from the Gunbarrel, the icefall just below the summit ice cap sweep. The Gunbarrel dominates the upper Linda area and the Linda Shelf and you must keep moving, like in the lower Linda, to lessen the chance of being caught by a deadly ice avalanche. From there you traverse the steep and exposed Linda Shelf to the gullies leading up to the summit rocks.

Once up and moving on the crampons a few things were very obvious — I was moving slowly, and wherever the snow had that damn breakable crust it hammered me. The stumps felt like they were walking on glass, and below the Gunbarrel is no place to go slow, let alone stop. Every five metres or so we would hit a bit of crust and every time I broke through, frequently dropping to my knees. Then I would need to pull myself up using the Leki poles, wrenching the stumps and cramping my forearms and stumps. Once upright I then needed to pull the leg with the crampon up and out of the hole. Putting the foot down again was agony. After a few steps the pain would settle in to become the background norm and I would just carry on.

One step then another, but none of the rhythm of old, none of the athletic elegance of bouncing around on those great legs, just a continual stumbling through a mist of pain with flashes of white-hot intensity.

All I could think was that after years of dreaming, planning and filming, the whole thing was going to crap because of me and my stumps. Not Wayne's leg design, the weather, or the conditions (sure they all contributed), but me. Having Whetu and Narly around just compounded everything, more people in the Gunbarrel going slow because of me — so I 'pulled the plug'.

I yelled (actually more sobbed) to Charlie, 'Time to stop, Charlie, we need to go back and get the camera chopper into Bowie Ridge.'

I dropped to my knees and chanted over and over again, 'It's not supposed to end like this.' I was inconsolable. It shouldn't have ended like that; it needed to end on top of Aoraki/Mount Cook, not at the start of the Linda Shelf where the real climbing begins. I always used to hate the walk in, or the drudge work before the real climb, and this time I not only hated it, it also wrecked me. Bugger.

As soon as I had made the decision to go back I really focused on getting down out of the avalanche debris as quickly as possible, but first I yelled up to Wayne (with Woody, 100 metres above) to carry on, we hadn't come this far for everyone to go home empty handed.

As we started down all I could think, through the rising pain, was perhaps I could have made it, but after the next few steps I knew I wouldn't have — Christ, the stumps hurt.

Finally we reached the flat area we had stopped at near the Bowie Ridge. A quick bit of radio chatter with Spoon down at Plateau and then a cold wait for the film helicopter.

Could I have walked back down the Linda? Probably, but slowly, and as you will have guessed, slow is not the deal, especially in heat.

After 10 minutes of lying there, the ice cliffs on Teichelmann's Corner started up an almost continual fusillade, with avalanches sweeping down over our tracks of the morning. Sitting there we assessed the escape routes available if an avalanche looked like heading our way, though for me the reality was I couldn't outrun a hedgehog, let alone an ice avalanche.

The comforting beat of Russell's helicopter, easing in with his style and perfection that instils great confidence. Sweeping down the Linda in the cosy comfort of Russell's Squirrel, only hours after painfully slugging up it, all I could think of was how I needed to explain myself, my failure when I re-entered the world. I knew there would be film crews waiting, probably at Plateau Hut even, all wanting to hear the excuses. The emotional pain I was feeling which was almost worse than the physical pain in my stumps, was all about how I had let so many people down.

I could face film crews, journalists, whoever, but not Anne, Chas, Charlie, Hamish, Don, Whetu, Narly or Spoon. I really didn't and don't care too much what others think except those I know and respect which makes any failure twice as hard.

With eyes full of tears and trying unsuccessfully to control my voice I climbed out of the helicopter at Plateau Hut, gave Chas a hug and headed to the sanctuary of the little tent.

Hiding in my tent was essential for a while, it was all about getting it out of my system, doing a bit of the grieving for what might have been and what actually happened, before I was ready to face the world. Mary (who had arrived with the helicopter that afternoon) spent 10 minutes quietly helping me to get everything in perspective, some balance back into my mind. It was still bloody hard to face up to Chas and the team, but half an hour later it was time to re-enter real life again.

Sitting in the sun watching the media helicopters circle the summit was fun but also reminded me that I would have a job to do very soon, facing the press. While everyone was telling me how well I did, I knew damn well that's not how I saw it or how many others would see it.

When the inevitable happened and the TV helicopter landed at Plateau Hut the big surprise was that Anne and Amanda were on board. It was superb to have them there, for so long they had only seen photos of the Plateau and Aoraki/Mount Cook close up, but you have to be there on the spot to truly appreciate the grandeur and scale. It was great to share the environment that is the Grand Plateau, even if it wasn't in the most positive of circumstances. I could see it was difficult for Anne as well, she knows how I hate to fail, how I hate to let people down, and I'm sure she knew that it wasn't over yet, which meant the family and I would have to go through it all again.

I'm continually astounded that I keep on learning huge lessons as I go on in life. That day in December 2001 reminded me that I am disabled and it has helped me understand how I live my life as a dichotomy between being able and disabled. I sometimes tend to forget both aspects, especially the disabled bit.

The flight back down to the village was a bit of a subdued affair. I knew that more press would be waiting, more TV crews to be bright and positive to, more people looking for an angle or spin to put on the failure. I did what I had to do and then it was time to pack up, say thanks to everyone and head home to Renwick.

We called in to Mum and Dad's on the way, and Mum could see very clearly that it wasn't finished. I think she had hoped that if I succeeded then it would be over and out of my system, but it was just the opposite, unfortunately for her.

Back home I had a deck to build, some stumps to heal and a bit of a holiday to take to heal the mind. The winery always shuts down for the

Christmas and New Year holiday season so everyone is guaranteed a break before the next vintage. Two weeks of deck building and riding the roads of Marlborough for a few hours each day saw me getting even fitter, and the stumps starting to heal from the abuse.

I was ready for the next attempt. It had to be soon — I needed to finish this sooner rather than later. I sorted and repacked my gear, and got the Vitara loaded up and ready to go at a moment's notice.

So it was back to checking the weather maps, with regular calls to Charlie. I was straining at the leash. That decision to turn back continually replayed in my mind, not because of any doubts but because it was one of the hardest things I had ever done. Just as importantly, the whole expedition was an experience to learn from: I had to do better with food and drink; I had to pick the conditions more carefully; or else I had to just walk away until I did get those things right.

9 FINISHING IT OFF

JANUARY 3rd 2002. EVERYTHING was pointing towards a weather window in two or three days' time. Time to assemble the troops and head south. Calls to Charlie, Whetu, Wayne and Chas to organise some support, to see who was available and keen to have another go.

This time no Hermitage and no media circus if I could help it. Amanda and I headed south, with Anne following a bit later. We drove down across the Canterbury Plains in a huge nor-west storm, torrential rain and an incredible hail storm as we were nearing the township of Mayfield. We were barely crawling along in poor visibility, the hail hammering on the Vitara's roof drowning out the stereo, and some of the hail stones bouncing almost a metre off the road. Out of the wall of hail appeared a red Mazda convertible, with the roof down. If you were the driver of the convertible, no offence, but Amanda and I laughed for hours.

This trip we were staying in the holiday home of Anne's brother, Steven, in Twizel. As soon as we pulled up the drive it felt right, this was more like me. I was keen to be down there, on the spot. There's only so much you can tell from weather maps and reports; experience and my own eyes are just as important. The first morning there, out on my bike, my feelings were confirmed. This time it felt dead right, more normal I guess. This time I really felt in control. When I'm out on the bike, an environment where I am 'elite' and feel confident, I feel like I used to while climbing — this is my space, my world. Early that morning riding up the Mount Cook road, the clouds cleared and Aoraki was there, towering above. My eye went directly to the summit and I knew I would be standing there very soon, that's how confident I was that everything would jell.

But by late afternoon both the clouds and a few nerves set in. It's always been like this before a climb, nerves about how you will perform, the weather, and for me, nearly always, what to take. It's a good sign that you are about to do something big, something that's not going to be easy. I must have looked at my gear and repacked it all a dozen times that afternoon trying to decide what to leave behind. Too many years as a scout, always being prepared, means I want to cover every eventuality on the hill — but then you have to carry the damn stuff. I didn't take quite enough gear back in 1982, and carried too much on my own back before Christmas, so was keen to get it right this time, or at least talk someone like Wayne into carrying it for me.

Anne felt far more at home in Twizel as well, rather than being left behind in the slightly artificial atmosphere of an international hotel (although Chris and Dennis at the Hermitage had done their best to almost adopt Anne, Lucy and Amanda). We all had a lot more confidence, and felt far more at home with the challenge ahead.

I spent a lovely evening sitting on Whetu's deck. The excuse was that we were doing a bit of planning, but we probably spent more time talking over old times and catching up with what people were up to. To be sitting there with Whetu and Charlie, sharing a wine, was one of the highlights of the year for me, though better was to come. Before Christmas everything was too hectic and intense to be able to relax in the right environment, just another sign I had got it right this time.

I didn't sleep much that Saturday night; I was probably even more nervous this time than the last. The night was spent getting up and down to the toilet with a rumbly stomach and I'm sure the only sleep I got was with one eye open.

Then it's 6 am, daylight brings cool cloudy weather, and it looks thick towards the Alps. I guess we may well be waiting for a hole to open. I hope that it's clear up high and plenty of parties are making their way up. The hut was going to be full again by all reports, and with the expected spell of good weather being the first for weeks, the mountain would be crowded.

The stumps weren't perfect: the right was fine apart from ever-worsening and spreading spots of psoriasis, but the left was a bit of a concern with an ulcer near the end of the stump and a new bit of wear resulting in some bleeding behind the knee. The psoriasis had developed slowly over the last few years, triggered by rising stress in my job, in life in general, I guess. Mostly it is confined to my elbows, but anywhere that takes a beating is susceptible. Psoriasis is just the body cycling the epidermal cells too quickly. Cells normally last for about 30 days, but when psoriasis graces you with its presence, they cycle in about two days, leaving red, raw and scaly flesh — not very picturesque and very annoying, but that's life. From what little I understand, drugs can't cure it and any that control it are just as bad for you as the condition.

Putting the cycling legs on was a bit of a trial, with the damage to the left stump. Like a lot of injuries to the stumps, it was very sore initially but it seemed to moderate after I'd been wearing them a while and after some movement. 'Oh well, here goes anyway.'

The standard morning call to Charlie: 'Hey the weather's great, mate, we have a window, let's go this afternoon.'

It wasn't quite that easy as we needed to assemble our team, the 'circus', and decide on whether it was worth Chas coming down to film from the air. My first thought was 'NO', I really didn't want the responsibility of Chas wasting a trip. Irrespective of the fact that the documentary was valid whether or not I made the summit, I knew I would feel a huge responsibility to succeed if they came down from

Auckland again. I knew it was his last chance to get footage before putting the documentary together to meet deadlines, and it would be my last chance for the summer season as well. I could start to feel the pressure straight away; I didn't want to be in the position of having cost him time and money if the weather turned bad or I didn't make it again.

The team was again Charlie and me, with Woody the safety for Whetu this time, as Narly was busy. Wayne had turned up at midnight after a marathon drive down from a shortened boating holiday in the Marlborough Sounds. Wayne's role on this trip was to be the 'camp bitch', the mechanic for the legs and sherpa for me.

I thought Chas and the cameras were staying away, but as the helicopter was being loaded in Twizel I heard Charlie being consulted on whether Chas would be in Twizel before midnight to fit up the helicopter with the camera. 'Oh well, in for a penny, in for a pound.'

It was time to concentrate on myself, my task, and not worry what

Loading the helicopter, Twizel, January 2002. From left: Woody, Charlie, Russell (pilot) and Wayne on the right.

was happening on the periphery. That was the mistake I had made the last time, and I wasn't going to fall into that trap again.

The plan this time was to do the Linda Glacier again, but to bivvy a night at the safe Bowie Ridge site. The weather was looking OK, so it would be a night out under the stars, in sleeping bags and bivvy bags. If the weather turned nasty we would need to head down to Plateau Hut, but there wouldn't be a climb if it turned that nasty.

We were packed and ready for the late afternoon trudge up the Linda. I could see in everyone a need for completion following the disappointment of Christmas time. I can't remember who suggested, 'Let's just fly into the Bowie and finish the bastard off,' but no one objected to the idea.

As soon as it was voiced there was a lifting of tempo. No one wanted to do the Linda again, not because of the walk, the sweat or time, but all of us (over 70 ascents of Aoraki/Mount Cook between us) had spent too many hours under the Linda ice cliffs to ever want to spend more hours there. Hell, we are a film crew anyway, so we *should* fly. I gave it a lot of thought as I knew the decision would create some controversy. The only reason to fly was to complete the documentary. I was there for completion, and to test out the legs in a difficult and technical situation. We were flying (as most climbers do) half way there anyhow, so a bit further, to just below December's high point just seemed logical.

What a flight, Russell is a master, the Squirrel just purred in his hands. Flying from Twizel up the lake was picture perfect. Aoraki stood bright in the sunshine, up above the low cloud ceiling. Every second up there, every kilometre closer, I knew this time we had it right, that I could do it. Landing in the Linda, under the Bowie Ridge, was like going home, a bit like coming back to a ski run you had fallen on years before but knew you could nail now.

What a fantastic place for a bivvy. When Russell flew off back to Twizel, the dense silence was shattered with the Teichelmann's Corner ice cliffs avalanching, cracking, booming like artillery. This continued for the rest of the afternoon and all night. Any residual guilt disappeared when we realised those avalanches were sweeping across the uphill tracks

Moving up the Linda Glacier towards Bowie Corner. From left: Woody, Whetu and Wayne.

we would have climbed. We walked up the glacier a few hundred metres, navigating around some of the huge ever-changing crevasses, and found a safe, level site for the bivvy. The engineers in the party started to shift the earth (well snow and ice), creating their sleeping benches, with Woody and Wayne becoming almost obsessive in the levelling of their sites. In contrast Whetu and I would have huddled up anywhere. The site was chosen predominantly for safety, protected from any possible avalanches by several very large slots that would swallow anything thrown at us.

The sun was frying us in seconds, you could feel the rays burning right through clothing and sunscreen. The heat was to be short-lived though, as you could see the shadow line advancing across the glacier towards us, with the sun disappearing over the Main Divide. The change in temperature was fast and dramatic, turning bitterly cold in minutes. Time to hide in the sleeping bags. Woody was designated chef in Narly's absence, and a brew was rapidly on the go. I wasn't too sure about his

At Bowie Corner: so pleased to be there.

culinary skills though when his creation for the evening was a mix of dehydrated roast lamb with vegetables and a Thai chicken in green curry. With my stomach still very tender it looked too much, the thought of trying to climb Cook with diarrhoea wasn't a pleasant thought for anyone, but I managed to rescue some lamb and veges before the meal became too international.

Charlie constantly had his nose to the weather, in fact I don't think 'the captain' slept that night. It was lucky we were sorted with our gear because the temperature dropped at least 20°C. It was like an instant freezer — bloody great. We listened to the park radio 'sched' at 7 pm, counting all the names in Plateau to get an idea of whose company and how many of them we would have the next day.

What a sky show that night. Stars in the mountains are fantastically bright, with so much reflective snow and ice around. You even get a clear moon shadow, totally magical. I haven't felt so at home in years. How I wished Anne and the kids could experience it.

There is something special about bivvying, even the food tastes different (better, luckily) and everything is far more real and alive and exciting. There is also something humbling about bivvying — you get to experience the true mountain, the soul of the thing. At times the mountain just toys with you, like that night; while at other times it turns nasty and throws everything at you, something everyone there that night had experienced at one time or another.

Soon after dark the clouds came over Green's Saddle under the high peak of Aoraki/Mount Cook, from the worst direction possible, the west. With the addition of an intermittent breeze that had sprung up, it was a very bad portent, something to make everyone a bit nervous. I could see Charlie with his nose and head out of his bag checking the weather even more often than I was — it was a neat feeling to know that someone else cared as much or more than me.

The idea was to be moving by 3 am, which should have been at least one or two hours before the Plateau Hut climbers would be anywhere near us, giving us a clear uninterrupted climb. Woody was going to do the stove, and make like the breakfast chef. That has to be the worst part of a bivvy, being the first person to have to stick your head out of the bag, let the cold air in, and do the fiddly job of lighting the stove in the dark without setting yourself on fire. I was sure that was why we had brought Wayne along but Woody decided to be the morning hero — I certainly wasn't volunteering.

When 1 am arrived the sky was clear and starry. Charlie and I both had our heads out and were thinking it was time to get going. The others had thought I was joking when I had said I wanted to go at 11 pm, but I never mind being early, especially here where much of the straightforward terrain is climbed in the dark, and I desperately wanted be above the 'crowds' that would be coming up from Plateau. I also wanted to be able to stop when I needed to, so as not to end up pressured

Woody and Whetu at 3 am, in the Bowie Corner bivvy: time to get up and make breakfast.

for time as happened during the attempt before Christmas. I didn't really get the message through at that time — and I still need to work on being more forceful, as this time we left a bit late (for me) and still didn't climb with the tempo that suited me.

Even starting to get ready at 1 am was too late, as by 3 am, when we were moving, there were at least nine or even more lights on the slopes around and ahead of us. The Linda was in good condition that night and most of the parties were leaving early and making good time. We went off at a steady pace, not the burst and stop that has typified the way I climb, as with ice cliffs still above us it was essential to keep moving steadily up and away from them. After about 30 minutes of climbing the ever-steepening slopes up underneath the 'Gunbarrel', which lead to the Linda Shelf, an English couple passed us with a cheery good morning. I asked one group we were close to, 'How was the Linda this morning? It sounded active —' (meaning dangerous, which it was). 'No problem,' they said. 'Safe as houses.' We knew then that we had some very green and inexperienced people around us.

In the dark we soon passed the December high point, a real relief. The snow conditions were variable, mostly good cramponing but there were pockets where I was still punching through into sugary snow on hard ice — far from perfect, but do-able.

The Linda Shelf was fun; I felt good and fit; it was dark so there was no problem with vertigo (it's bloody steep and exposed). Once out from under the ice cliffs we had our first brief stop, taking on some food and fluids. My drink, in its bladder in my pack, had frozen to a slush: quite drinkable but a bit chewy. The whole sipper tube had frozen making that 'good' idea pretty useless. This trip I made sure I wasn't relying on somebody else's food (like the PowerBars that froze solid making them inedible on that first climb) and I had a plentiful supply of my own sports gel. It is a unique recipe I have worked on for several years, perfecting a chewy gel that gives you a real burst of energy and life, while still tasting like a great espresso.

The climbing up the shelf was mostly front pointing for me, almost crab-like movements on a long rising traverse. A few small slots appeared here and there but little to worry about as long as I concentrated on tool and feet placement. Near the top, the shelf flattens out a bit just before the first real obstacle, the Linda Shelf bergschrund, a big crevasse high on a steep slope with an overhanging lip to negotiate. We stopped here for another brief break, after ploughing through some deep snow just below the 'schrund. Daylight was on us, so it was time to pack the head lamps away and get some cream on in preparation for the sun that was coming. There aren't many things higher than you up there, and the dawn is always impressive looking north over the Southern Alps. About three other parties were crossing the 'schrund 50 metres away, so with a bit of a queue forming where they were, we decided to find another crossing point. To me it looked as though we picked the hardest place to cross the slot — so much for going with guides. 'Well, pick the hardest place to cross, why don't you, guys? Let's start the challenge here, shall we?'

The idea was to get away from the queue and it worked for about 10 minutes until we entered the couloirs under the summit rocks and started to get a pounding by ice from the groups above. This lasted the next four hours or more. Above the 'schrund the usual route is up a broad couloir to the ridge line, up the narrow arête until it merges with the face of the summit rocks. We were climbing relatively fast (certainly for a gimp anyway), passing some of the other groups as we front pointed up in mixed ice and hard snow conditions. There was some good firm ice which made for lovely firm front pointing, mixed with some sugary snow over hard ice, a bit harder for me to feel comfortable on. The DMM crampons I had chosen and Wayne had modified were great in the firm ice but lacked bite on the very hard ice and sugary snow.

With people climbing above, there was no shortage of debris cascading down onto us. It was mostly ice from where the other parties were cutting belay stances and knocking off lumps around exposed rocks.

The film helicopter appeared for the second or third time then as well, reminding us of the outside interest in the climb and of what I considered my responsibilities. But 'bugger off' was probably the most common sentiment of everyone on the mountain at the time. People were starting to get a bit aggravated, with the crowding on the tight pitches meaning queuing for a line to climb, and the intrusion of the helicopter didn't help. It didn't hang around long each time, which was good, but it would be back.

While all this was going on I was thinking, 'Yeah, I really am back climbing,' though I was looking enviously at Charlie, Whetu and Woody — those guys move with such grace and assurance. It's something to aim for, to get back to a skill level where I can be comfortable on slopes like those, where I can move with safety and assurance, just like I do already in my head.

Every step, every move, every tool placement, brought back memories of my old technique, and after every move I knew I could do the next one better: a fantastic feeling.

Charlie was in full guide mode, telling me not to worry about falling, not to place my tools so hard ('Don't overdrive your tools, Mark') as he had me on belay, so it wouldn't matter if I fell.

Like hell. Once a mountaineer, always a mountaineer, and you sure don't fall unless things are really on the limit.

'Yeah yeah yeah, Charlie, I know I'm overdriving the tools, but mate, no matter what, I AM NOT GOING TO FALL OFF THIS MOUNTAIN WITH A CAMERA UP MY ARSE.' I think he understood.

So, after 20 years, I was back at the first pitch of the summit rocks, although this time they were almost fully iced up. Back in 1982 we hadn't come up this way, although we were planning to descend that way to Plateau via the Linda Glacier. The last time I had been here was probably at least a year before that on my Grand Traverse or on one of the Zubriggens route climbs. The first 10 metres was mixed technical ground, a traverse and small step but with lots of exposure, mixed rock and ice footing and holds. The Linda Glacier route is technically the hardest part of the whole ascent of Aoraki/Mount Cook because of the combination of technical steep mixed ground and the very serious consequences of any fall, due to the exposure. We arrived at this bottleneck just as one party disappeared up over the first step: more ice cascading down, but mixed with rocks this time.

The client in the guided party in front of us was nervous and a novice climber. The pitch was obviously a major challenge to him (and me) and I had to watch him claw his way up. Charlie shepherded him up, advising him on holds, calling out to his guide, Caroline, to have a tight rope as he looked pretty shaky. Just before the crux move, when he was swapping from axe placements to hand holds, he dropped his ice hammer. Now someone with the skills of Whetu, Charlie or Woody might feel at home with only one ice tool on these steep couloirs and ice steps, but this guy certainly wouldn't. The tool bounced down a steep ice couloir for a few metres and stopped. But before any of us could retrieve it a large lump of fall ice hit it and away it went again, somersaulting down about 10 metres until burying its pick in some softer snow. Woody down-climbed to one side of it, careful not to knock the ice hammer the rest of the way down to the Linda or into a slot, and brought it back up to the start of the pitch. Charlie then climbed up to the poor sod just past the tricky traverse in the pitch and delivered it with some useful hints about hanging onto his gear. This wasn't what I'd wanted to see before I climbed the pitch, certainly not what you would call inspiring for my first really technical pitch on a big mountain in 19 years. Somewhat cockily though, I did think that I'd be pissed off if I made that much of a hash of it. The reality was that my passion to do stuff perfectly meant that although I was a bit gripped (mountaineering term for scared shitless) at first, I did some good moves and felt the biggest rush in years. It is those first few moves after standing still that are the hardest. We had to wait probably 15 minutes on a small stance for Caroline and her client to climb the only line and get clear, enough time for anybody to stiffen up, but even worse for my stumps. Just standing, and especially when stuck on a small foothold, is bloody hard on the stumps, because there is no relief from the pressure as when you are walking or climbing. Sometimes even sitting down is very uncomfortable. It does take a while for the stumps to feel settled and firm.

Charlie moved off, and I noted that even he was treating these moves with respect. He quickly disappeared up out of sight, climbing past Caroline's client. After what seemed an age the rope stopped paying out and the 'on belay, Mark' call came down from Charlie.

The moves started with a sidle along an icy ledge, with some of the ice underfoot on the ledge breaking away because of the crampon traffic that had already gone over it. Holds were a mix of 'dry tooling' (where you use your ice tools to hang off rock holds, a pretty freaky feeling at first), a bit of ice for the tools to bite into securely, and a handy jug or crack type of hold for the hands here and there. I surprised even myself with a few opposing hold moves, just like rock climbing at home, 'cool' I thought, the real thing and the juices were flowing. With a tricky step up and around a bulge onto a steep ice slope and then up a short vertical step, the crux was dealt to. What remained was just over two rope lengths of steep ice, a series of linked couloirs with short vertical steps in between.

As soon as I was half way up that pitch I was fizzing, it was in the bag, just time now and some serious sweat, so I started to really enjoy myself. The worst thing about those two pitches was being constantly hammered by ice and rocks from the climbers above. I caught a nasty bit of ice in the face and a fist-sized rock on the arm, but who cares, I HAD DONE THE CRUX.

I knew then that nothing could stop me, although my right crampon almost did. Those moves through the crux pitch had pushed the right crampon back on the foot, making front pointing with that foot a bit of a mission. The DMM crampons weren't working as I had hoped. I am reliant to a large degree on the downward force, my weight, to get them to bite into the hard ice, but they weren't doing it. Having to hammer them in with a kicking motion would trash my stumps quickly, so for the last pitch of the summit rocks I had to use the inside two points, making progress just a bit slower and more awkward.

Heading up the summit icecap, just above the summit rocks.

I started to get a bit of cramp in my forearms, a sure sign of overdriving (as Charlie had said), and also of the greater reliance I put on the ice tools because of the crampons and the fact I'm a double amp.

There were moves on the summit rocks that had me quite gripped at times, especially when ice and rocks were cascading down. Five or six times I had to stop, hanging off my ice tools, shoulders hunched, as debris rained down, hitting my helmet with loud cracks and thuds. I pictured all those times in the months before when people would ask: 'Is there snow at the top of Mount Cook in summer?' Yes, there certainly is, although a lot of it was knocked off and landed on me that day.

Coming over the top of the summit rocks, you need to drop down a wee bit of hard ice to a col at the bottom of the ice cap. Looking up the ridge to the summit I could see a burning-hot trudge to come, interspersed with fluffy snow over hard ice. I thought, 'You can see the end, but there is a lot of sweat to lose first!'

Charlie was, as always, concerned about the time, but I kept thinking that I didn't care. Hell, even if it took me another three days to get down, as long as I was off the summit rocks by dark, I was happy. I could spend a couple of nights at the Bowie Corner bivvy site, rather than wreck myself and my stumps.

After the first few metres up the slope, Charlie was burning up in the direct sun, so we stopped to lose the jackets. I dithered about a bit (and slowed them down again) but took mine off as well, giving it to Woody to carry for me.

Off again on the trudge, the first 150 metres a steep sidle up near the ridge line, the edge of the summit ice cap, in knee-deep snow with hard slippery ice under it. I had the choice of plugging new steps, which would have been very tiring, or trying to make use of the steps already formed. This was a nightmare at times, just like before Christmas, with the steps right at the limit of my leg mobility, and crampons that weren't biting into the ice as they should. But I could see the top, so the ice cap was very much a case of toughen up and hurry up. Just 150 metres below the top, on the steepest section, we struck harder ice again and went back to pitch climbing for over two rope lengths. Caroline had kindly left her belay anchors in for us, making life easier and quicker.

I was head down and going for it, the top was near and the sooner I was up, the sooner we all could start the journey down. The last belay point was just below the 'Chandelier' (the mushroom-shaped ice bulge beneath the summit) so as soon as Charlie yelled 'on belay' and I looked up, I could see him standing on the top, and things started getting misty behind the glasses. I remembered telling Chas that part of this climb was to avoid sitting at home crying on November 29 any more, and I thought, 'Bugger, now I'm going to do it every time I remember these few metres.'

That last 30 metres was a whirlwind of emotions, I was smiling so much I thought my face would crack. 'Christ,' I thought, 'you have to do this regularly just to feel the buzz.' When I had climbed before, once I made it to the top, the question was usually: 'How on earth do I get back down?' This time I wasn't even giving it a thought. If necessary I would crawl — hell, it's all downhill anyway.

Those last 30 metres disappeared in a blink. My mind was going so fast, thinking continuously of the past, especially of before Christmas. There were thoughts of Anne and the kids, thoughts of, 'Nothing can stop me now, I can do anything eventually.' Passing Whetu in the last couple of steps, all I could think of was, 'Stumpy and Gimpy on top of New Zealand — how about on top of the world next?'

I'd forgotten how hard it was to stand on top of a peak like that. I wasn't really feeling all that stable, and I was thinking, 'I'll look like a bloody old man stooped over like this, stand up, man.'

Charlie had me on a short rope for the last few metres along the summit ridge to the compromise bump that's called the summit these days. A few hugs, ham it up a bit for the helicopter camera and it's almost time to be off. I kicked myself for not putting my jacket on before stepping up there; I was cooling down rapidly. We got Woody to do a few summit photos with our cameras, then back down below the Chandelier to prepare for the descent.

The grins were huge on every face there, as they are with every ascent of Aoraki/Mount Cook. The buzz is always there, even for those for

Celebrating with Charlie on top of Aoraki/Mount Cook.

whom climbing it has become a job. For me there was also the relief, and almost disbelief at how great it felt to be back. I was conscious of the debt I owed to every person who helped me there, but also very conscious of the personal achievement and a rising desire to go higher and harder.

Standing there, just like on the podium at Sydney, was the start of something, not the end of something.

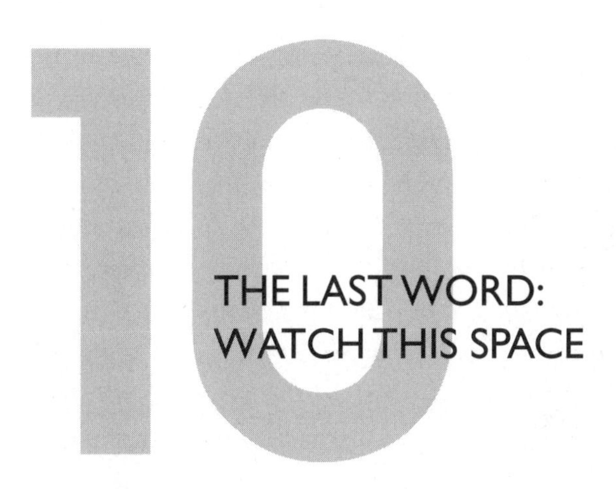

10 THE LAST WORD: WATCH THIS SPACE

GOING DOWN MOUNTAINS IS always an anticlimax, but this time I was taking with me two things that would last forever: I had had another chance to stand on top of Aoraki/Mount Cook, and, even more importantly, I had lifted myself up to another level.

To speed up the descent, Charlie, Whetu and Woody set up a double rope lower, which, on slopes where the guide can down-climb with safety, is quicker than abseiling down. In minutes I was down to the col (the climber's term for a dip in a ridge, like a pass) at the base of the ice cap. Whetu 'arm-rapped' down the rope (running down the steep slope with the rope wrapped just around your arm, rather than around your body or through a belay device as used on steeper slopes), and Woody and Charlie cleaned the anchors and gear off the mountain while climbing down. At the time we thought it strange that no one had come up behind us, we were the last people on the ice cap that afternoon, the other teams below deciding it was too dangerous to come up. By this time it was just after 2 pm. The steeper the ground the easier it was for me. The places that posed the biggest problems for me when coming down the ice-cap were the 'flatter' bits, as I was wading and stumbling in deep snow, crampons balling up very badly. The stumps were starting to take a bit of a hammering, especially as I was getting a bit dehydrated from the heat of battling the deep snotty snow. I could feel a few tears, a bit of skin missing to be sure. The other issue was that after 12 hours on the go, the stumps' sockets were drenched in sweat and would have 'packed down'. The socks become thinner through dampness and compression, which means a sloppy fit with less precision of foot placement. In all, we were all getting a bit buggered. In film crew mould again, the rationale was, we've got what we needed, so out came the radio and we ordered up the helicopter to pick us up above the summit rocks, pick up Wayne and the gear 750 metres below, and head home to Twizel.

Cheating? Only if you were going to claim an 'ascent' I guess. Hell, I just wanted to do the really hard bits; the boring bits can wait until another time.

Back in Twizel the atmosphere was of quiet achievement, of completion, although I knew some would see what I had done in a negative light. That night we celebrated with a barbecue at Charlie and Mary's home, as you do, a few wines and beer. I was being careful to keep moving as I had done some damage to the stumps, but it's also really important to let the muscles wind down and recover actively, so a few miles on the bike were what the doctor ordered.

We all watched the news channels avidly, as Chas had released some shots to TV1 while TV3 had their own camera in the air that day (one of the helicopters that people were to complain about later). We were keen to see what sort of spin each channel would give the item. I was really concerned about the way they would portray the event, worried they would be crediting me with the first 'paralympic' ascent, rather than just presenting my desire to summit again. I had given interviews freely to ensure that I could get the correct information across, but even that didn't diminish the sensationalist approach.

From my point of view I had done something pretty damn hard, but not something to be idolised for. I'd have been more than happy to have a few lines in a newspaper — or none at all. As I had told everyone, I did it for myself, it seemed like a damn good idea, an adventure with a pioneering element and a great story to tell people, to show people what ability is and how it is within everyone.

But anonymity wasn't to be, in fact just the opposite, and with the intense news coverage came the detractors. First the conservationists, complaining that I should not have done it the way I did, as we had caused significant disruption to the wilderness nature of the alpine environment. Then 'members of the climbing community', who protested at the amount and type of publicity I was receiving when I hadn't actually 'climbed' the whole mountain.

By 11 pm that evening what had been a fantastic adventure that would show New Zealanders what their backyard was truly like, had been turned into a session of sour grapes by many. But for every detractor, many more supporters came forward over the next weeks. It seemed as though the timing was all wrong and a group of people with differing agendas all ended up using me as a political football. I rapidly got sick of it. I made sure my story was told as clearly and as truthfully as possible to reputable journalists but some still continued to find the negative in my accomplishment.

June 2002

Back home in Blenheim I have quickly become aware of how much my life has changed, not just because of climbing Mount Cook again, but because of the direction I have been pushing myself in ever since that summer in California in 1997. Back then, by stepping outside my routine life in New Zealand, I think I reawakened that urge for change that has always been part of my makeup, but only surfaces occasionally.

It was the time over there, seeing the wealth of experiences and life outside our small community, that was the driving force for me to look to the Paralympic cycling movement. It was through that movement, and the mentoring of people like Ben Lucas at Parafed, that I was able to realise my dream of competing with success at the Paralympics.

Standing there on top of Aoraki/Mount Cook again, the thing I treasured most was that I had made the journey back, not necessarily to the mountain itself but the journey back to the real people, the life that the mountains encompass. The waves of emotion all centred on freedom, and the assurance that it is time to do something big, something else.

The mountains can be a curse in that they make you see your true self. That's something that we often try hard to do, and we enlist all sorts of specialised help, when all you really need to do is challenge yourself, and for me that happens in the mountains.

I used to do it for my living, for my life. I used to help others get the chance to do it as well, and it is only now that I understand that the buzz from helping others is as great as doing it yourself.

Whenever you come out of the mountains, especially after pushing yourself to the limit, you have a wildness in your heart, a drive and freedom that wasn't there before. You know you can achieve things that were once only a dream. And the more times you undertake the extreme journey, the greater your confidence becomes that you will attain your dream and the bigger your dreams become.

I have always had a fascination with individuals who attempt extreme endurance sports, especially the Race Across America, the RAAM. The competitors ride their cycles for nine days virtually non-stop, they push their bodies and minds to, and past, any previously defined limits. There is little fanfare or public idolisation, little monetary reward, but the freedom they experience afterwards is like a licence to excel and achieve.

My 'RAAM' is a Kaitaia to Bluff ride, as close to non-stop as my stumps, body and mind will let me. Like Aoraki/Mount Cook, this isn't about an obsession, it's about an adventure, a challenge. It will be six or seven days of my life that probably won't be all that pleasant. On trips of that magnitude you start out nervous and excited, then the hard work starts, and the realisation of what you have committed yourself to sets in and you enter into a serious mood. As you acclimatise to the adventure, the trip becomes a pure delight, and some time around then you hit the the high point. You can never plan for when it will be, or for how long it will last, but when you get there you know that is what it is all about.

AMP will support me as they have done in many of my adventures, and we aim to raise awareness of ability and also, along the way, to raise funds for a charity that will benefit children.

Even bigger, of course, is Mount Everest. The top of Aoraki/Mount Cook has a lot to answer for. Standing there with Charlie, Whetu and Woody, the unspoken dream always in my unconscious came to the fore. Mount Everest — Norman Croucher and Ed Hommer (both double amputees, Ed missing just his feet, Norman, an inspiration to me from day one) have both almost done it. What an adventure that would be. Once again, not an obsession, because that's one of the things that kills you on Everest. The whole Mount Cook team are showing as much if not more enthusiasm for it than me, so we hope that May 2004 will see Charlie, Whetu, Spoon, Woody, Narly and me all on top of the world.

To get to the top of Everest takes work, it isn't something that can be brought as many have found out and it isn't a place to trial new techniques, legs or old bodies. To maximise our chances of success, we are going first to Mount Shishapangma in Tibet during April and May of 2003. 'Shisha' is just above 8000 metres in height, much easier on the body than Everest and an excellent test of how each of us will cope at altitude. While the climb of Shisha is quite straightforward, skiing off the top will surely add some spice and it will sure beat walking down, always my nemesis. Shisha will also be a great chance to travel with my family, a chance to share some of the secrets and adventures of the mountains with those that I love.

To do these adventures will take a significant amount of time, more time than a senior winemaker at Montana has available, so I must part company with the other family I have spent my last 10 years with, Montana Wines. The reality is that for the last year my heart has been elsewhere and winemaking is one of those 110 per cent jobs; if you aren't giving it that level of commitment then you are just making a beverage, not that living thing, wine. To be fair to Montana, myself, my family and my health I have said goodbye to a salary and have struck out with that self belief that I'm cursed with.

The next two years will be full of adventures and challenges. To keep bread on the table I am taking my story and the lessons I have learnt to New Zealand sports clubs, boardrooms and schools, sharing with people my passion for participation in life. I am lucky that I have now got a bag full of skills from years of learning in a range of environments, a bag of skills that I now have to turn into a living.

My last months at Montana have seen me daily asking myself, 'Why the hell am I leaving, the future here is astounding,' followed by, 'Let me out of here.' While we had a small grieving ceremony over the disappearance of my salary, it is like being let off a leash, like having a lid removed from above your head, from above your ambitions.

I guess each time you push yourself you learn that much more about yourself. You come out with a greater respect for your body, for the things it can do and how you should look after it so it will do even more.

You come out with a greater respect for your mind, for the barriers it can overcome. The real trick in life and adventures is marrying everything together, the body, the mind, the preparation, your responsibilities to yourself and others, so you can achieve a result that is worthy of the effort.

They say that success breeds success and that is probably true, but I believe that the desire to challenge yourself breeds the desire to further challenge yourself, and that brings success and, more importantly, achievement, which I think is the essence of life.

I am often asked what I want out of life, what I want to leave behind. These are very complex questions, but, simply, I want to provide in every way for my family and I want to 'make a difference'.

The next years will see adventures, will *hopefully* see me showing people how *they too can* make a difference in *their own way*.

Come along for the ride.

Mark Inglis
June 2002